STEPHEN CRANE'S

LOVE LETTERS TO NELLIE CROUSE

Stephen Crane, 1893, by C. K. Linson

STEPHEN CRANE'S
LOVE LETTERS
TO NELLIE CROUSE

with six other letters, new materials on

Crane at Syracuse University

and a number of unusual photographs

EDITED

WITH NOTES AND INTRODUCTIONS

by EDWIN H. CADY

and LESTER G. WELLS

SYRACUSE UNIVERSITY PRESS

1954

to

GEORGE ARENTS

whose love of books

has greatly aided this one

PREFACE

The contents of this volume are presented by the editors, one of whom is the Curator of the Stephen Crane Collection of Syracuse University, as an earnest of the continuing concern of the University and its family of faculty, alumni, and students for the memory of a great American author who was, however briefly, part of it. The editors are well aware that theirs is far from the last word on Stephen Crane. They are confident, however, that when the last word is written the Crane materials in this book will play their part in determining what is said. The Crane letters here, like much of the supporting evidence, have never been published before. So far as we can learn, none of the very interesting photographs has ever been published either.

The following acknowledgments for assistance in making the contents of this book available are made to:

George Arents for his gift to Syracuse University of the seven Crane letters to Nellie Crouse (1895–1896); his letter from Lafayette College (1890); his letter to L. L. Button (1892); his letter to C. K. Linson (1895); his letter to W. B. Hawkins (1895); his letters to Copeland and Day (1894–1895); his letter to Karl Knortz (1895); his letter to James Pinker (1899); Cora Crane's letter to unidentified publisher (1900); Raymond J. Wheeler, Jr., for permission to print Crane's letter to Viola Allen (1896). The library of Columbia University for permission to print C. J. Little's letter to Crane (1899) and

Frank Smalley's letter to Cora Crane (1900). Syracuse Chapter of Delta Upsilon for permission to print Crane's letter to O. S. Hathaway (1891). Alfred A. Knopf, Inc., for general permission to print the letters. Florence Crane Coughlan and to Edmund H. Crane for their cooperation and interest. Corwin Knapp Linson for photographs reproduced herein and for the inspiration and assistance he has extended to the editors. Edith Carpenter Lundgren (Mrs. Sven R.) for the photograph of her mother, Nellie Crouse, and for the invaluable help she has extended in enabling the editors to write concerning the letters written by Crane to her mother.

Syracuse, New York
April, 1954

CONTENTS

PICTURES

1 SIX LETTERS TO OLD FRIENDS

ONE
To a Claverack College Schoolmate

Either third or fourth in order among the earliest known of Crane's letters, this was written in a bold, curving, immature hand on four pages of cheap notebook paper to a schoolmate left behind at "old C.C."—Claverack College—of which see more in the introduction to the next letter. Crane had registered at Lafayette College on September 12, and Thanksgiving came on November 27 in 1890. "A hell of a time at C.C." apparently meant adolescent orgies of beer and tobacco in a village poolroom. But Crane spoke with some authority when he boasted that "the fellows here raise more hell than any college in the country." One Lafayette freshman baseball player had made unpleasant headlines by beating up a hazing sophomore with a baseball bat; and Crane himself, scared but defiant, had stood off a raiding party with a revolver [L. U. Pratt, "The Formal Education of Stephen Crane," *American Literature*, X (January, 1939), pp. 466-68].

(Between September 12 and November 27, 1890)

My dear boy,

Your letter gladly recd. So you are not having a hell of
a time at C.C., eh? Well, you had better have it now because, mark my words, you will always regret the day
you leave old C.C. The fellows here raise more hell than
any college in the country, yet I have still left a big slice
of my heart up among the pumpkin seeds and farmers of
Columbia Co. You asked me if I thought as much of Pete
as ever. Well, I should think so, and a great deal more besides, and don't you forget it. We both may possibly come
up on Thanksgiving and you fellows whom I still love as
of old, must give us a jolly time. So long, old man, don't
forget me even if I can't be at C.C.

Yours, as ever

Stephen Crane

#170 East Hall
Lafayette College

TWO

To Odell S. Hathaway, January 9, 1891

Hathaway, whose son, Odell S. Hathaway, Jr., presented this
letter to the Syracuse Chapter of Delta Upsilon, was Crane's
classmate at the Hudson River Institute and Claverack College,
Claverack, New York, which Crane entered in February 1887
and left to attend Lafayette College in 1890. Claverack was

coeducational but military. Crane wore a uniform and drilled a squad there. But baseball and dating (see his letter to Viola Allen below) absorbed his major interest. At Lafayette and then at Syracuse whence he transferred in January 1891 he was a fiendishly enthusiastic baseball player (for a survey of his relations with Syracuse see Appendix I below).

Hathaway, who did not go on to college, owned and managed a chain of theaters in New York and Ohio but died in 1934 without having the chance to screen *The Red Badge of Courage* or "The Bride Comes to Yellow Sky."

"Sioux" was Earl T. Reeve the "Rushville Indian" (cf. *Stephen Crane: an Omnibus*, ed. Robert W. Stallman, New York, 1952, p. 590) because he came from Rushville, Indiana.

"Travis" was Abram Lincoln Travis, Syracuse '94, who taught at Claverack in 1894-95 and established the Travis Classical School in the city of Syracuse.

"Brusie"—Sanford Brusie, like many of the men then at strongly Methodist Syracuse University, became a Methodist clergyman: which helps account for the fact that the "fellows" were "somewhat slow."

My dear Hathaway,

Those pictures have not come yet and neither has any letters from the little crowd of tough devils who hang out in Sioux's room. I ate like a fiend as soon as I got away from Claverack and am eating like a devil now, every chance I get. What has Harry had to say to you since I have been gone? Has he jumped on the mob any more? If he has, damn him. The ΔY Chapter here has got a dandy house valued at $20,000.00, situated on a high hill overlooking the entire city. I hope you may all come here

sometime, although the fellows here *are* somewhat slow.
Yet, . . . [portion of letter missing] . . . As I said before
to Sioux, there are certainly some dam pretty girls here,
praised be to God. Not as nice as they as [*sic*] are in
Newburgh, however. There is where the dandy girls are
found. Gene has got an awful big belly on him, but he is
the same old Gene as of old, good-natured, jolly and so-
ciable. Travis still keeps his same military step that he
once used with such success in H.R.I. Brusie is just such a
chap that he was; hard, dry, cold and calculating. . . .
[portion of letter missing] . . . [This is a] dandy city at
least and I expect to see some fun here.

Well here is where I must stop. Give my love to everyone in the old crowd and don't forget this poor devil.

Yours always

Stephen Crane

Delta Upsilon Chapter House
Syracuse, N.Y.
Jan 9th. 1891.

THREE
To Lucius L. Button [December 15, 1892]

On February 5, 1853, Dr. Frederic M. Lawrence of Carlisle, Pa., a fraternity brother of Crane's at Syracuse, wrote to Lester G. Wells in part as follows: "Stephen Crane was my most intimate friend for the several formative years which followed our meeting in Syracuse. I had cut short my college career to enter the medical school in New York and "Steve" came along. Crane's brother was a successful attorney in Port Jervis (Lawrence's home) and "Steve" and I had become closest of friends. There was scarcely a day or an evening which we did not spend together. When I went to New York to study medicine Crane went along . . . we occupied the principal room on the second floor overlooking the East River and distant Brooklyn and it was there that Crane did most of his earlier work. In addition to ourselves there were perhaps half a dozen other medical students in the boarding house, and at Crane's suggestion we assumed the title of the 'Pendennis Club.' . . . Lucius Button, fresh from Yale, was one of the 'crowd' and was well liked."

Button, whom Crane called "Budge," had apparently known Nellie Crouse in Akron. Crane joshed him about the "intolerable duffer" from Akron whom he met in New Orleans in 1895 (cf. Stallman, pp. 612-613), and it was Button who took Crane to the tea on 34th St. at which he met Nellie Crouse. He became Dr. Lucius Lucine Button of Rochester, N. Y., after his medical graduation in 1895.

L. L. Button and Stephen Crane (left to right) 1893, on roof of Linson's studio, West 30th St., New York City.

Pendennis Club
1064 Eastern Boulevard

My dear Button:

I was glad to be made aware by your genial pen that the dragon is sad because I have escaped her. But if she be vindictive, I will have my revenge. I have had a dog given me. And I am seriously thinking of inflicting it on our admirable land-lady after Christmas. It is a mere little fox-terrier with a nose like a black bead and a pedigree as long as your arm. It evinces a profound tendency to raise the devil on all occasions, which it does, mostly, by tearing up gloves, and wading around in any butter plate, mince-pie, or cake which it may perceive at large. It also has a violent antipathy to larger dogs, cats, and all fowls of the air. Withal, it is a meek little thing when in human presence and keeps it's black, white and tan coat spotlessly clean. If I can prevail upon our dear, domestic tyrant to let me pay it's board, I shall certainly bring it down after Christmas. I adore dogs. I think I shall be again at the Pendennis Club tomorrow night to see you fellows before you all hie away for Christmastide.

I am gratified that you remembered me by your note of this evening and, meanwhile, I remain, my dear boy,

Yours always

Stephen Crane

Lake View, N.J.
Wednesday.

8   SIX LETTERS

FOUR

To Corwin Knapp Linson [February 19, 1895]

Headed merely "New Orleans, Tuesday" this must have
been written on February 19, since the Mardi Gras on "next
Tuesday" took place February 26. Crane was on his trip to the
Southwest for the Bacheller Syndicate. Corwin Knapp Linson
(1864–) met Crane in 1892 when Linson was an art student at
the National Academy of Design. Crane haunted his room on
West 30th street, often virtually living there, and it was on
Linson's battered sofa that Crane began *The Red Badge*. The
humor of the letter is, of course, generically Crane.

Mon ami Linson: Friedweller die schonënberger [*sic*] je
suis dans New Orleans. Cracked ice dans Nebraska, terra
del fuego dans New Orleans. Table d'hotes sur le balconies just like spring. A la mode whiskers on the citizens
en masse, merci, of the vintage de 1712.
    Frequented I all the time here again l'etoile de Virgini-
tie sur St Louis Street. Sic semper tyrannis! Mardi gras
tres grande but it not does until next Tuesday begin.
Spiel! Senger to me one letter wrote filled with abuse. Ce
matin I write un article sur le railways du South which
were all made in hell.
    This boarding-house est le terrible Francais. I have
learned to ask for the vinegar at the table but otherwise
I shall perhaps to Heaven go through starvation.

                                                    Yours ever

New Orleans   Crane
Tuesday

"Stephen Crane and C. K. Linson on roof of my studio, West 30th St.,
1893"—Per C. K. Linson

FIVE

To Willis Brooks Hawkins, October [24], 1895

The image of a Bowery-haunting, Bohemian Crane has too
often obscured that of the out-doors man and lover of fine
horseflesh who wrote from rural Hartwood. Hawkins apparently succeeded Dr. Lawrence as Crane's most intimate friend
(cf. Stallman, p. 618 and the fine speech recorded by Frank W.
Noxon in Appendix I, below). He was editor of the Brains Pub-
lishing Company and a Lantern Club mainstay.

Book publication of *The Red Badge* had occurred in September. In September Crane was in Philadelphia, then in New York in early October, not returning to Hartwood before the latter half of the month. On October 23 he wrote Hathaway that he had missed his first partridge that day (Stallman, p. 624).

Hartwood, Sullivan County, N. Y.,

My dear Willis: The brown October woods are simply great. There is a kitten in the stables who walks like Ada Rehan and there is a dog who trims his whiskers like the late President Carnot's whiskers. Gypsey, cousin to Greylight and blood relative of the noble Lynne bel, who lost the Transylvania so capably at Lexington this season— well, Gypsey ran away with me. What can be finer than a fine frosty morning, a runaway horse, and only the still hills to watch. Lord, I do love a crazy horse with just a little pig-skin between him and me. You can push your lifeless old bicycles around the country but a slim-limbed thoroughbred's dauntless spirit is better. Some people take much trouble to break a horse of this or that. I don't. Let him fling himself to the other side of the road because a sumach tassle waves. If your knees are not self-acting enough for that sort of thing, get off and walk. Hartwood scenery is good when viewed swiftly.

I missed my first partridge yesterday. Keh-plunk. Bad ground, 'though. Too many white birches. I haven't written a line yet. Dont intend to for some time. Clip anything you see in the papers and send it. Remember me to everybody at Greene Ave. I have heard indirectly from Brentano's that the damned "Red Badge" is having a very nice sale.

Yours as always
Stephen Crane

Oct. '95

SIX

To Viola Allen, March 15, 1896

The solidity of these reminiscences of flirtations at Claverack shed some light on Crane's preparation for his siege of Nellie Crouse's heart. The gaiety of them makes it difficult to take the gloom of the March 1 and 18 parts of the seventh Crouse letter with entire, melodramatic seriousness.

The Cosmos Club

Washington, D.C.

My dear Miss Allen: I am very glad to be able to forward you by this mail a copy of The Red Badge. My years at Claverack are very vivid to me. They were I believe the happiest period of my life although I was not then aware of it. Of course, you were joking when you inferred that I might not remember you And Anna Roberts! And Eva Lacy! And Jennie Pierce! Alas, Jennie Pierce. You must remember that I was in love with her, madly, in the headlong way of seventeen. Jennie was clever. With only half an effort she made my life so very miserable.

Men usually refuse to recognize their school-boy dreams. They blush. I dont. The emotion itself was probably higher, finer, than anything of my after-life, and so, often I like to think of it. I was such an ass, such a pure complete ass—it does me good to recollect it.

Yours sincerely,

Stephen Crane

March 15th, 1896.

Mon ami Lomson : Friedwelley die schweinbergeye sind dans New Orleans. Cracked ice dans Nebraska, terra del fuego dans New Orleans. Table d'hôtes, sur le balconies just like spring. A la mode whiskers on the citizens as usual, merci, of the vintage de 1712.

Frequented I all the time here again. l'étoile de Virginie an St Louis Street. Sic semper tyrannis! Mardi gras très grande but it does not does until next Tuesday. Begin. Sfin! Senqer to me one letter white filled... write un article sur les railways du South which were all made in hell.

This boarding-house est le terrible Tram-cars: I have learned to ask for the vinegar at the table but otherwise I shall perhaps to Heaven go through starvation.

Yours ever
Crane.

New Orleans
Tuesday. 95

II THE CROUSE LETTERS
OF STEPHEN CRANE

INTRODUCTION

Sometime, presumably when Crane was in New York in January 1895, arranging for the publication of *The Black Riders*, a young medical-student friend, Lucius L. ("Budge") Button, took him to a tea on 34th St. to meet old friends from Akron, Ohio. Like all pretentious occasions, the tea paralyzed Crane. But his imagination, naturally susceptible at the age of twenty-three to charming women, was intensely stimulated by a willowy, *spirituelle*, but very chic beauty whose talk challenged him there. Her name was Nellie Janes Crouse (see Appendix 2), and her impression remained vividly with Crane even through his Western and Mexican adventures during the ensuing spring. Apparently that image did not dim while *The Black Riders* in May and then *The Red Badge of Courage* in September brought him first a wry notoriety and then explosive international celebrity. For on the last day of the year he seized some handy pretext and wrote her, maneuvering skillfully to capture her interest. Then in eager succession through the rest of the winter he wrote to her the longest, the most intimately self-probing, and perhaps the most important of all his letters.

Ever since Mr. Jerre Mangione first wrote about the Crouse letters in the Syracuse University *Chap Book* in 1930, there has naturally been great interest in them on the part of Crane students. They were then held for sale by a bookseller in Rochester. By 1944 they had come into the hands of Mr. Benjamin Swann, then of the Swann Auction Galleries, New York, who sold them to James F. Drake, Inc., of the same city. Thence they were acquired by Mr. George Arents, who in June 1950

generously presented them to the Stephen Crane Collection of
the Syracuse University Library, under the auspices of which
the present publication is made.

It is not difficult, after studying them, to say that these are
love-letters, the love-letters of an unusual man in a slightly unusual situation. As Nellie Crouse's daughter, Mrs. Sven R.
Lundgren, testifies (Appendix 2), it was a family tradition that
Crane was in love with her mother and even, a fact not re-
vealed by the letters, that he actually came to Akron to see her.
Remembering that Crane had only seen his lady once before he
began to write, a quite coherent picture emerges when one considers the strategies of his letters. At twenty-four Stephen Crane
had a thorough and normal knowledge of the opposite sex. As
a prep-school and college student he had been sharply aware of
pretty girls and enjoyed his part in adolescent courting skir-
mishes, as his letter to Viola Allen in this volume makes clear.
Subsequently he had been, worshipfully and hopelessly, in love
with Helen Trent, already engaged, and Lily Brandon Munroe, already married. Nellie Crouse, though geographically distant, was imaginably much more available; and Crane went to
work to intrigue her as she had him.

The first letter is carefully calculated to win a friendly re-
sponse. Shamelessly using "inside" reactions to his celebrity to
impress, it also stalks behind an aura of exotic settings and gay
humor to tell her how impressed he is. If nothing else, he will
claim the right of a reply to know "where Button is at." How
could she help replying if she liked him at all? Having won his
reply, and apparently a good one, he raises the temperature of
the correspondence eagerly in his second letter. Without los-
ing the chaffing note traditiony for the early stages of court-

ing in the group to which both he and she belonged, he becomes more intimate. He offers to confess—"if it ruins my egotism for a fortnight." He angles for an invitation to come to
Akron. He even volunteers to accept her literary advice!

The third letter opens the heart of the correspondence from
Crane's side. Telling her, lover-like, "I understand you perfectly," he begins seriously to try to make her understand him.
His deepest knowledge is opened to her; he explains how less
than nothing his celebrity means to him; he states and, again
lover-like, tries sequentially to account for the "curiously potential attraction" her image exerts upon him. The strategies of
his fourth letter suggest that the previous one was perhaps too
serious, too quickly intimate, that she has reacted coyly, and
that, while bowing to her maneuver, he is determined to brush
it aside. Skilfully he plays to capture her again, brilliantly at-
tacking the clichés of the celebrity system, sketching himself
trapped in "the social crisis" and dismayed equally by celebrity
and social women. In all this Crane has the advantage of being
sincere as well as "different"; he makes his point by being himself and so makes it well. If he is true, however, he is not ingenuous. The general discussion leads to the particularity of
his meeting her and so he forces an opening to return to his
basic question. Recklessly and insistently he throws himself on
her imagination. Here, firmly and openly, is his best thought,
his ultimate conviction and knowledge about human life. "Will
she respond?" he asks tacitly. Is she *the* woman who will perfectly understand and sympathize? The tragic, and the roman-
tic, desire of all men somehow to be perfectly received lies at
the bottom of his declaration. It is not really surprising that
Nellie Crouse could not respond as he unspokenly hoped.

But she did respond enough to send her picture, and the fifth
letter, returning to the acceptable tone, expresses jubilation and
worship. Also it proposes, with much less pressure than in the
two previous letters, the posture of a relationship then thoroughly conventional. She is so wonderful—"I am awed . . ."—
but he is "admittedly a savage": won't she take and make him
over? The sixth letter, however, is a sudden reversal of that
convention; perhaps she took his "savagism" too seriously. She
said something about admiring "the man of fashion" and elic-
ited a disquisition which may be startling to readers of Crane
who have accepted too facilely the facts that he lived Bo-
hemianly for a while and did pioneering imaginative work
about the Bowery. It is a well-informed, hard-hitting, highly
coherent, surprisingly complete survey of the problem of the
ideal of the gentleman as it stood in Crane's time. Basic to
Crane's own thought and to his books in ways we shall see
later, this was also basic to his courting. For Nellie Crouse's
picture joins with the strategies of Crane's handling of her to
suggest that she was indeed a woman after Crane's own heart.
She was chic, fundamentally tough-minded as well as clear-
thinking, and independent. Beautiful and effective in her charm,
she knows she can choose among men. Crane, descendant of
the Cranes of New Jersey, is out to prove how thoroughly he
belongs as well as understands. And yet, at the end, he insists
on a return to the ideal: Tolstoi shows the way.

Whatever happened after that, whether Crane went out to
Akron to get his dismissal between February 11 and March 1
or not, the atmosphere of the first part of letter seven is different. For the first time in the Crouse letters the writing has
become consciously literary, displaying the famous Crane images

and color-words to convey his rather formal feelings of despair
and self-pity. The two sentences added on March 18, while
brief, are very effective—and equally literary. The affair is
over, and the correspondence with it; he has had his *congé;* and
he leaves her with the final word, for twinge or thrill as her
case may be, that life is now only "a mouthful of dust."

It is not easy to name documents more significant to an un-
derstanding of Stephen Crane and his work than these letters
to Nellie Crouse. His wished-for definitive biographer will find
important new side-lights upon his character, his self-concept
of that character, and the working philosophy to which his
experience of living had brought him. It is no surprise to find
Crane independent of the world, defiant and ironic against its
stupidities, hypocrisies, and vulgarities. His integrity, both personal and artistic, is a familiar part of the legend. But it is new
to find him so controlled, so perfectly aware both of his youth
and of his age, his perennially astonishing wisdom and preco-
cious power. The newest thing, however, is the depth of moral
discrimination and conviction lying so explicitly open here. It
has always been implicit in his best work, of course. But our
knowledge derived from reading a literary work is often subject to doubt and disputation. There can be no question about
this now.

What the Crouse letters suggest is the basis for a theory of
Stephen Crane. Child and heir of the Cranes, a religious New
Jersey aristocracy (of a culture now buried under Suburbia as
deep as Herculaneum), he had become a radical, unchurched,
defaithed, Christian gentleman. Joseph Conrad saw the facts
when he stressed Crane's chivalry, and courtesy, and sensitivity.
Trained to believe in the great tradition of the Christian gen-

tleman as it had been Americanized in the generations of Jef-
ferson and Emerson and Robert E. Lee, Crane made the tem-
peramentally natural gesture of taking it seriously. Then, much
like Henry James, Sr., he was moved in the name of the ideal
to revolt desperately against the smothering conventionalities
of moralism and respectability by which the world evaded the
ideal. "If the road of disappointment, grief, pessimism, is followed far enough," he pointed out to Nellie Crouse, it will arrive
at "the final wall of the wise man's thought . . . Human Kindness." The resultant morality and piety of pity, sympathy, and
open humility had been that, as Crane probably did not know,
of Hawthorne and Melville. As he might have seen, it was the
message of Mark Twain's masterpiece, *The Adventures of
Huckleberry Finn*. As he probably knew well, and as the reference to Tolstoi at the end of the sixth letter suggests, it was
the creed of the latter, Tolstoian William Dean Howells who
was his friend. Classically it is the conclusion of *King Lear*, the
lesson drawn by the battered king on the stormy heath and implicit in his final observation, "ripeness is all." Human ripeness
sees pity and kindness as "the final wall of the wise man's
thought." We shall probably never know what made Stephen
Crane so ripe so young.

It is probably not necessary to point out that these attitudes
had much to do with the character of Crane's literature. The
quest for an absolute vision which is related both to his philosophy and the method of his art had much to do with the in-
dividualities of language, subject-matter, perspective, and sym-
bolism he achieved. His disillusionment with conventionalities
made the ironies of *Maggie*, "The Monster," *The Red Badge*
and "The Open Boat," to say nothing of the poems and the

other tales, possible. His idealism made admirable the heroism of Billy Higgins, the oiler, and of Doctor Trescott (of "The Monster"). His ethics of pity and kindness reached out empathically to give substance to all his best people and their symbolic actions. It is the dominant quality of his imagination as it was of his thought.

Nellie Janes Crouse, 1872–1943
Photo taken Akron, winter of 1896, supplied by her daughter, Mrs. Sven
R. Lundgren, 1953

ONE

To Nellie Crouse, December 31, [1895]

A great deal of miscellaneous material on the Philistine Dinner, including an appreciation of Crane by Elbert Hubbard, may be found in *A Souvenir and a Medley: Seven Poems and a Sketch by Stephen Crane*, East Aurora, N. Y., 1896. Stallman reprints a series of letters from Crane to Willis B. Hawkins (pp. 631-643) recording his immediate reactions to the Philistine occasion. See also the dramatic account of the dinner by Frank W. Noxon in Appendix 1 below.

Hartwood, N. Y.
Dec. 31st

Dear Miss Crouse: I embrace with pleasure the opportunities of the walrus. I knew little of the Philistines until they sent me this letter:

East Aurora, N.Y., Nov. 10, 1895.

To Mr. Stephen Crane:

Recognizing in yourself and in your genius as a poet, a man whom we would like to know better, The Society of the Philistines desire to give a dinner in your honor early in the future. If this meets with your approval we should be glad if you will let us know upon what date you could conveniently come to us.

Elbert Hubbard.
H. P. Taber, Editor of the *Philistine*.
Samuel G. Blythe, of the Buffalo *Express*.
Wm. McIntosh of the Buffalo *News*.
Eugene R. White of the Buffalo *News*.
Philip Hale of the Boston *Journal*.

Nelson Ayres of the New Orleans *Picayune.*
L. H. Bickford of the Denver *Times.*
Marshall Cushing of the Washington *Capital.*
Walter Blackburn Harte of *Moods.*
John Northern Hilliard of the Rochester *Union and
    Advertiser.*

COMMITTEE for The Society.

I was very properly enraged at the word "poet" which
continually reminds me of long-hair and seems to me to
be a most detestable form of insult but nevertheless I
replied:

Hartwood, N.Y., Nov. 15, 1895.

To Mr. Elbert Hubbard, Mr. Harry P. Taber, Mr.
Eugene R. White, Mr. Wm. McIntosh, Mr. Walter
Blackburn Harte, Mr. S. G. Blythe, Mr. John North-
ern Hilliard, Mr. Philip Hale, Mr. Nelson Ayres, Mr.
L. H. Bickford, Mr. Marshall Cushing, of the Society
of the Philistines.

Gentlemen:

The only obstacle in the way of my accepting an
invitation at once so cordial and so kind is the fact that
an acceptance, it seems to me, is a tacit admission of my
worthiness in the circumstances. Believe me, this sense
of embarrassment that I should be at all considered as a
fit person for such distinction is my solitary discomfort.
But I have industriously blunted this sense and can say
that it will deal me great pleasure to dine with the Society of the Philistines on Thursday evening, Dec. 19th.
    I beg to thank you, gentlemen, and pray believe me
that I am ever

Very Sincerely Yours,

STEPHEN CRANE

I am convinced that I would have written a worse letter if I had had the slightest idea that they were going to print it. I went to Buffalo and this is not at all what happened:

THE PHILISTINES AT DINNER.

Their First Banquet Was Given Last Night at the Genesee In Honor of Stephen Crane.

The Colonial parlor of the Genesee was the scene of an interesting gathering last evening. The "Society of the Philistines," as the literary men interested in the "periodical of protest" and some of their friends rather ambitiously term themselves, met to do honor to Mr. Stephen Crane, author of "The Black Riders" and some other striking verse, and "The Red Badge of Courage," a book of prose dealing with our civil war which is exciting widespread interest just now. Mr. Crane is unquestionably a Philistine, according to the definition of the society, for he writes what pleases him, in his own way and takes all the chances of its pleasing any one else. The purpose of the Philistines is to encourage just such independence and individuality in literature and other matters and Mr. Crane was thus in the house of friends though personally known beforehand to none of the Philistines here. It was at first intended to have the dinner at East Aurora, the habitat of the Philistine magazine, but for the convenience of many who came from out of town a more central meeting place was found.

Besides Messrs. Harry P. Taber, editor of the Philistine, and Elbert Hubbard, his associate and neighbor at East Aurora, there were Philistines from many points away from Buffalo. The visitors included Mr. Claude Favette Bragdon, the well-known artist and architect of Rochester, who has become known through his work in the Chap Book and the Philistine as "the Beardsley of America," though a very positive critic of the affectations of the Yellow Book School; Robert Murat Halstead of New York, editor of the Fourth Estate, a son of "Field Marshal" Murat Halstead; Col. Robert Mitchell Floyd of New York, Willis B. Hawkins of New York, Robert C. Adams of Scranton, Livy S. Richard of the Scranton Tribune, A. J. McWain of the Batavia News, John Northern Hilliard of the Rochester Union and Advertiser, George P. Humphrey of Rochester, Frank W. Noxon of the Boston

Chicago, and Dr. A. L. Mitchell of East
Aurora. The others present were Messrs.
E. R. Lawrence, Buffalo manager of the
Associated Press; Samuel G. Blythe, Fred
W. Kendall, John O'Brien, Clifford A.
Wibert, David Gray, Harry Kidd, Philip
Becker Goetz, Frank O'Brien, J. H. Ham-
ilton, Ben F. Coe, E. R. White, Dwight R.
Collin, Wm. McIntosh, C. A. Friedman,
Herbert L. Baker. There were 31 in all
and every seat was filled. Regrets were
received from many notable men in the
literary world, including Charles Dudley
Warner, Chester S. Lord of the Sun, Wm.
Dean Howells, Frank Dempster Sherman,
Maurice Thompson, L. H. Bickford of the
Denver Times, Ambrose Bierce, Gillett
Burgess of the Lark, San Francisco; Bliss
Carman, Hayden Carruth, Walter Black-
burn Harte, Robert W. Criswell, John L.
Heaton, Edward W. Bok, Charles F.
Lumniss, Richard Harding Davis, Hamlin
Garland, E. St. Elmo Lewis, Louise Imo-
gen Guiney, George F. Warren, Daniel
Appleton and Amy Leslie of the Chicago
News.

Mr. Taber presided and acted as toast-
master and Mr. Hubbard from the opposite end of the table made the address
of welcome to the special guest of the
evening, who sat at Mr. Taber's right. He
traced the story of the Philistines, who, he
said, had had the worst of it in all times,
because a tribe of invaders of their country, who had been slaves in Egypt, "had
the pull with the publishers" and the narrative of Palestine told only one side of
the story. Later Matthew Arnold, repre-
senting the colleges and the culture of
England, and having a pretty heavy bur-
den to carry, had bunched all critics and
opponents of what he professed in one
category and called them all Philistines.
He went on the vindicate the apostles of
sincerity and personal independence, and
closed with an eloquent tribute to the
"strong voice now heard in America,"
the voice of Stephen Crane.

Mr. Crane responded modestly and grace-
fully, saying he was a working newspaper man who was trying to do what he
could "since he had recovered from college" with the machinery which had
come into his hands—doing it sincerely, if
clumsily, and simply setting forth in his
own way his own impressions. The poe
made a very good impression. He is
young fellow, 24, with a smooth face and
keen eye and doesn't take himself ov
seriously.

Informal addresses by many others
lowed, the most notable being a state
by Mr. Bragdon of what some Phili
in art are trying to do in cultivatin
cerity of expression in every form
He lightly but effectively dealt w
pretensions now given the old r
who, he said, never took themse
seriously as their worshipers n
and advised his hearers to be not to

However it is one man's idea of what happened and not altogether wrong in proper names. I had a good time and caused them considerable trouble in inventing nice things to say to me.

I do not suppose you will be overwhelmed with distinction when I tell you that your name is surrounded with much sentiment for me. I was in southern Mexico last winter for a sufficient time to have my face turn the color of a brick side-walk. There was nothing American about me save a large Smith and Wesson revolver and I saw only Indians whom I suspected of loading their tomales with dog. In this state of mind and this physical condition, I arrived one day in the city of Puebla and there I saw an American girl. There was a party of tourists in town and she was of their contingent. I only saw her four times—one in the hotel corridor and three in the street. I had been so long in the mountains and was such an outcast, that the sight of this American girl in a new spring gown nearly caused me to drop dead. She of course never looked in my direction. I never met her. Nevertheless I gained one of those peculiar thrills which a man only acknowledges upon occasion. I ran to the railroad office. I cried: "What is the shortest route to New York." I left Mexico.

I suppose you fail to see how this concerns you in anyway! And no wonder! But this girl who startled me out
of my mountaineer senses, resembled you. I have never
achieved the enjoyment of seeing you in a new spring
gown but this girl became to me not an individual but a
sort of a symbol and I have always thought of you with
gratitude for the peculiar thrill you gave me in the town
of Puebla, Mexico.

The lives of some people are one long apology. Mine
was, once, but not now. I go through the world unexplained, I suppose. Perhaps this letter may look like an
incomparable insolence. Who knows. Script is an infer-
nally bad vehicle for thoughts. I know that, at least. But
if you are not angry at me, I should like you to tell me
where Button is at. I lost him almost a year ago and I
have never been able to discover him. I suppose it is his
size. He could be so easily overlooked in a crowd.

Yours sincerely

Stephen Crane

TWO

To Nellie Crouse, January 6, [1896]

The Philistine published Crane poems in August ("Chatter of
a death-demon"), September ("Lantern song"), December
("Slant of sun on dull brown walls") 1895; January ("I have
heard the sunset song of the birches") but not again until June
("Fast rode the knight") 1896.

"Hitchy" Hitchcock of Buffalo we have not identified. Ripley Hitchcock (1857–1918) was literary advisor of D. Apple-

ton, 1890–1902. Crane's many dealings with him probably began with *The Red Badge*, first published in book form by Appleton.

The Gray Sleeve was published serially in the Philadelphia *Press*, October 12, 14, 15, 1895. The *English Illustrated Magazine* published it in January 1896.

Hartwood, N. Y.
January 6th.

Dear Miss Crouse: Of course it was my original belief that you would not be offended at my letter. I had formed a much higher opinion. If you had rushed out and defended your dignity when it was not assailed, I would have been grievously disappointed. I felt that I was doing something unusual but then I believed I saw in your eye once that the usual was rather tiresome to you. I am galloping all around the point of the argument but then—you know what I must mean—and it is awfully complimentary.

I am sorry that you did not find the "two poems"—mind you, I never call them poems myself—in the *Philistine*. No more did I. But as a matter of truth, the *Philistine* will have something of mine in every number in 1896 so if you ever see that little book again this year, you will on search discover the lost one. I never encourage friends to read my work—they sometimes advise one —but somehow I will be glad to send you things of mine. Not because I think you will refrain from advising one either. But simply because I would enjoy it—sending them, I mean. I think your advice would have a charm to it that I do not find in some others.

I observe that you think it wretched to go through life unexplained. Not at all. You have no idea how it sim-

plifies matters. But in your case I make humble conces-
sion and I am prepared to explain anything at all which
I can find power to do. I have been told 84676 times that
I am not of the cream of mankind but you make a sort
of an inference that I might myself think I was of it, so
I hasten to say that although I never line the walls or
clutter the floors of ballrooms, my supreme detestation is
dowdy women although they may be as intellectual as
Mahomet. If you had seen me dashing through the back
streets of Buffalo to escape the Browning Club, you
would believe me. I am not sure that they were very anxious either, but then I was anxious, and I would not have
been caught for a great deal.

When you said that Hitchcock mentioned me, I was
alarmed for I thought you meant Ripley Hitchcock of
New York and I knew just how he would mention any-
body save himself and God. I resolved to overthrow him
on the first opportunity. But then I perceived that you
meant Hitchcock of Buffalo. His name, you understand,
is Hitchy. If you had said that Hitchy mentioned me, I
would have known at once.

I am sending you by this mail a newspaper clipping of
"A Grey [sic] Sleeve." It is not in any sense a good
story and the intolerable pictures make it worse. In England, it comes out in a magazine and if I had a copy I
would send you one, in order to make you think it was
a better story but unfortunately I have not yet seen the
English periodical.

I must here candidly say that I am not insanely de-
sirous of knowing Button's location. Originally, it was a
pretext. But still I am glad to know that you know where
he is and I would be glad to have you find out for me,
for he is as good an Indian as ever lived.

I am not very much on newspaper work now but in
the spring I am wanting very much to go to Arizona to

study the Apaches more. There is a man in Boston who
has been unwise enough to ask me to write a play for his
theatre and I wish to have some Apaches in it. For instance the music of their scalp dance is enough to set fire
to a stone church. And in this connection I intend going
west on the Erie. This route leads through Akron, as I
distinctly remember. Furthermore,—if I don't go to Arizona—I shall at any rate go to Buffalo and if you will
please tell me that Akron is not far from Buffalo, I will
make an afternoon—or possibly evening—call on you.
Sure.

I am deeply interested concerning that lot of things
which you say you wish to know. I pledge myself to
" 'fess" if it ruins my egotism for a fortnight. Anyhow,
it is a very comfortable and manful occupation to tram-
ple upon one's own egotism. When I reached twenty-
one years and first really scanned my personal egotism
I was fairly dazzled by the size of it. The Matterhorn
could be no more than a ten-pin to it. Perhaps I have
succeeded in lowering it a trifle. So you will please keep
in mind that there is a young [missing word] corduroy-
trousered, briar-wood smoking young man—in Hartwood, N. Y. who is eagerly awaiting a letter from you.

Sincerely yours,

Stephen Crane.

THREE

To Nellie Crouse, January 12, [1896]

Crane did not die as he was "minded to" in his thirty-fifth year, of course, but in his twenty-ninth on June 5, 1900. His opinion of reviewers had not been brightened by the fate of *Maggie*, which was ignored by the book-publicity machine in its first, virtually private, printing, nor by the stupidity with which *The Black Riders* had been received in spite of cordiality from William Dean Howells and the *Nation* (see Thomas F. O'Donnell, "A Note on the Reception of Crane's *The Black Riders*," *American Literature*, XXIV, May, 1952.) The magnificent English reception of *The Red Badge*, his first transatlantic publication, was a new and decisive experience. He was called superior to Zola and Tolstoi and even compared to Sophocles.

The "new novel coming out in the spring" was probably the Appleton publication of *Maggie* in June. Though McClure had hesitated and lost *The Red Badge*, he was now, of course, intensely interested in Crane.

The "awful chump" whom he cautiously questioned about Nellie Crouse (to get just the right answer) was the "duffer" he had pilloried for Button the previous March (Stallman, pp. 612-613).

Hartwood, N. Y.
January 12th.

Dear Miss Crouse: How dreadfully weary of everything you are. There were deeps of gloom in your letter which might have made me wonder but they did not, for by the same token, I knew of them long ago. As a matter of

truth, I learn nothing new of you from your letters.
They merely substantiate previous opinions.

For my own part, I am minded to die in my thirty-
fifth year. I think that is all I care to stand. I don't like to
make wise remarks on the aspect of life but I will say
that it doesn't strike me as particularly worth the trouble.
The final wall of the wise man's thought however is Human Kindness of course. If the road of disappointment,
grief, pessimism, is followed far enough, it will arrive
there. Pessimism itself is only a little, little way, and
moreover it is ridiculously cheap. The cynical mind is an
uneducated thing. Therefore do I strive to be as kind and
as just as may be to those about me and in my meagre
success at it, I find the solitary pleasure of life.

It is good of you to like "A Grey [sic] Sleeve." Of
course, they are a pair of idiots. But yet there is something charming in their childish faith in each other. That
is all I intended to say.

When I implored you to advise me, I knew very well
you would not. But still I was crushed to an infinite degree when you suggested that I should take knowledge
from the reviewers. Oh, heavens! Apparently you have
not studied the wiles of the learned reviewer very much
or you never would have allowed yourself to write that
sentence. There is only one person in the world who
knows less than the average reader. He is the average reviewer. I would already have been a literary corpse, had
I ever paid the slightest attention to the reviewers. It may
seem to you that I take this ground because there have
been so many unfavorable reviews in America. Take this
then from England:

> The "Red Badge of Courage" has fascinated England.
> The critics are wild over it, and the English edition has
> been purchased with avidity. Mr. Crane has letters from
> the most prominent of English publishers asking for the

English rights to all of his future productions. [news-
paper clipping]

Now I have never taken the trouble to look up a single
one of these English reviews although I hear from all
sides how enthusiastic they are. As for the English publishers I wrote them that I remembered thinking The
Red Badge a pretty good thing when I did it, but that it
had no attractions for me now and as for any other books
I had not then the slightest knowledge of being able to
write them. So, you see if I despise reviewers it is not because I have not received favorable notice in some
quarters.

I am dejected just now because I have to start for New
York tonight and leave the blessed quiet hills of Hartwood. McClure is having one of his fits of desire to have
me write for him and I am obliged to go see him. Moreover, I have a new novel coming out in the spring and
I am also obliged to confer with the Appleton's about
that. But I am hanged if I stay in New York more than
one day. Then I shall hie me back to Hartwood.

Why, in heaven's name, do you think that beer is any
more to me than a mere incident? You don't, as a matter
of fact. You were merely warning me. Teas bore me, of
course, because all the girls gibber. But then you didn't
mean that I might run into a regular tea.

Of course, I knew of the young man who wrote the
back-hand. Not that he wrote a back-hand; but then I
knew that he had come and gone. Writers—some of them
—are dreadfully impertinent about knowing things. Once
upon a time there was a young woman but her sister
married a baronet and so she thought she must marry a
baronet, too. I find it more and more easy to believe her
stupid. This is rather lame consolation but I have known
it to work.

Your admission that many people find you charming, leads me to be honest. So prepare. I called once in 34th St., when you were there, didn't I? Well, I was rather bored. I thought you very attractive but then I was bored, because I had always believed that when I made calls I was bored. However to some sentence of mine you said: "Yes, I know," before I had quite finished. I don't remember what I had said but I always remembered your saying: "Yes, I know." I knew then that you had lived a long time. And so in some semi-conscious manner, you stood forth very distinctly in my memory. In New Orleans I met a fellow—awful chump—who said he was from Akron, O. After a decent interval, I mentioned my meeting you. I was delighted to find that he knew you. I said you were very charming and ultimately he said "rather queer girl, though." Of course he said you were charming, too, but then the slightly dazed manner in which he said "rather queer girl" impressed me. He apparently did not understand you and he being such a chump, I thought it a very good sign. You know the Mexican incident. It was very strange. When I arrived in New York I called at once at 34th St. Nobody was there. Long afterward, I sent the menu of that dinner at Buffalo.

There is the whole episode. You have been for me a curiously potential attraction. I tell it you frankly, assured that no harm could come from any course so honest. I don't know what it is or why it is. I have never analyzed it. Couldn't. I am bound to let my egotism have swing here and tell you that I am an intensely practical and experienced person, in fear you might confuse the word "poet" with various kinds of crazy sentiment.

I have said sometimes to myself that you are a person of remarkably strong personality and that I detected it in New York in that vague unformulating way in which

I sometimes come to know things; but then I don't even
know this. In short, I want to be frank but I don't know
precisely how. One thing however is certain. I would
like to know you. And when Akron becomes possible to
me, I shall invade Akron.

You will feel embarrassed. I'll bet on it. Here is a
young man who proclaims an admiration of you from
afar. He comes to Akron. You don't care either way but
then you feel a sort of moral responsibility. Great Scott!
What a situation!

The Bookman next month is I believe going to use a
photograph of me which is worse than one in the Chicago *Echo*. It is worse because it looks more like me. I
shall expect an answer soon. You have not yet told me
where is Button. I enjoyed your last letter immensely
and understood your point-of-view exactly. I am going
to take this letter to Port Jervis with me tonight so that
your answer may come quicker.

Very sincerely yours

Stephen Crane

FOUR

To Nellie Crouse [n. d., probably late January 1896]

Every student of Crane has justly complained of the cavalier
disdain with which he omitted or, worse still, mistook dates. It
seems clear from the internal sequence of ideas as well as from
Crane's insistent eagerness to get on with the correspondence
that this must fall between #3 of January 12 and the next dated
letter of February 5. The Lantern Club held a dinner for Crane

on April 7, 1896. But the "toast" they drank to him must have
been an incident of another affair because, leaving other consid-
erations out, not even Crane could in April have mourned the
fact that his proposed trip to Akron would be in "February
weather" and prevent his going riding with Nellie Crouse.

"One Dash—Horses" had appeared in the Philadelphia *Press*,
January 4 and 6, 1896.

What Crane sensibly called the "Lantern" pretentiously
called itself "The Lanthorne Club." Young journalists and as-
piring writers, among them Irving Bacheller, Richard Watson
Gilder, Willis Brooks Hawkins, and Ned Townsend, were the
members, and they idolized Crane for having fulfilled their
dreams of glory. Irving Bacheller, the president, explained their
activities atop an ancient building near the Brooklyn Bridge
as follows:

> The shanty on the roof was occupied by an old Dutchman,
> who gladly gave up possession for the sum of $50. Then the
> organizers, among whom was Stephen Crane, employed a cook
> and fitted up the shanty so that it looked like a ship's cabin.
> There, far above the madding crowd, the 'Lanthornes' held
> high intellectual revels. A luncheon was served every day,
> and the members let their hair grow long and their minds
> grow high. Every Saturday night they held a literary banquet.
> Each week some member of the club was assigned to write a
> story, and it was read at the dinner. Encomium and favorable
> criticism were prohibited. After the reading of the story the
> members jumped upon it as hard as they could, pointed out
> the flaws in it and pooh-poohed it generally, if possible. The
> highest tribute that a story could receive was complete silence.
> That was the best any writer ever got. [*The Manuscript*,
> Vol. I, No. 2 (May 1901), pp. 32-34].

Dear Miss Crouse:

I am just this moment back to the hills. I was obliged
to go down to Virginia from New York and so the time
of my little journey was unduly prolonged. I was impatient to get your letter and so had it forwarded to
New York where I got it two days ago but was so
badgered with silly engagements that I did not really
own a minute in which I could reply. Sometimes people
revenge themselves for delayed letters by calmly delay-
ing the reply but I know you will not treat me to any
such injustice.

I told you indeed that I was a practical and experienced person but your interpretation in this last letter
was perhaps a little too wide. I did not say so to "warn"
you. I mentioned it in a sort of a wonder that anyone
so prodigiously practical and experienced should be so
attracted by a vague, faint shadow—in fact a young
woman who crossed his vision just once and that a considerable time ago. This is the thing that makes me wonder. Your letters, however, have reinforced me. I know
much more of you now than I did before you amiably
replied to my first letter and I know now that my instinctive liking for you was not a mistake.

I am afraid you laugh at me sometimes in your letters.
For instance when you speak of a likelihood of being
aghast at being left alone with such a clever person. Now
that is really too bad of you. I am often marvelously a
blockhead and incomparably an idiot. I reach depths of
stupidity of which most people cannot dream. This is
usually in the case of a social crisis. A social crisis simply
leaves me witless and gibbering. A social crisis to me is
despair. When I am really myself however, I am all right,
being a good fellow, I think, and quite honest and simple. On most occasions I contrive to keep myself that

way but sometimes the social crisis catches me unawares. The "Great Scott" in my letter was intended to show me stupid, witless, gibbering, despairing when I meet you in Akron. I only wish it could be in riding weather. I could bring some togs and I dare say I could rent some kind of a steed in Akron. My pilgrimage to the west via the Erie will please me immensely if it achieves a ride, a tea and *An Evening Call*, in Akron. Considering February weather, I can forego the ride. The story "One Dash—Horses," which I sent you celebrates in a measure my affection for a little horse I owned in Mexico. I just thought to tell you. I was about to say however that you must submit to my being quite serious over the stop-off at Akron. As sure as February appears you can expect to be bored by *An Evening Call*.

I have some friends departing for London on the 29th of February and as some people in London have requested me to come over and be looked at and as S. S. McClure, Limited, has requested me to go to London for him, I am mildly tempted, but expect to decline. Travelling is a great deal of trouble. If however you have in mind any new excursions to the land where all bad newspaper articles come from, you ought to let me know for then I would feel capable of overcoming my inertia.

You don't mean to soberly say that you thought I was anything but very ordinary when I called in 34th St.? I was sure that on that occasion I was stupid. In truth I sometimes secretly wail over the fact that women never see the best traits of a man—not, at least, in our conventional intercourse. Many a duffer shines like a sun and many a brave man appears a duffer. To offset this, women have a sort of an instinct of discovery. Still I am sure that no women—not even the women who have cared for me—ever truly knew the best and worst of me.

There are three men in this world who know me about
as I am but no woman does.

I see that I am in danger of wandering. I meant to say
that in all social situations I am ordinarily conscious of
being minute. At a dinner the other night in New York—
the Lantern Club—they drank a very kind toast to me and
to see all those old veterans arise and looked [sic] solemnly
at me, quite knocked the wind from me and when it
came my turn to get up I could only call them damned
fools and sit down again. They were all old friends. At
Buffalo however where everyone was strange, I was as
cold as iced cucumbers when I arose and I said what I
had to say very deliberately. The social crisis catches me
sometimes and sometimes it doesn't. At Buffalo however I
didn't talk as well as I could talk and to a woman I never
talk as well as I can talk. Now that is exactly what I mean.
And I never made a call, fought a tea, or sat on the sands
by the mournful sea, that I didn't come away much dis-
contented. So, you see, when my mind recalled the evening on 34th St., I was always disgusted for I distinctly
remembered that I was more than usually stupid on that
occasion. And this is why I was bored then. It wasn't
because I didn't know I was meeting a very charming
girl, because I did know it. It was simply because it was
my experience and, later, my habit to be bored when
calling. Button, good a soul as he is, only dragged me
forth on that call because he was exhibiting his literary
friend. You know what I mean. It seems that to some
men there is a mild glamor about their literary friends
and they like to gently exhibit them. I was used to it and
usually submitted as decently as possible. It is awfully
nice to be exhibited like a stuffed parrot. They say that
Davis enjoys it. I should think he would. He has, I believe, the intelligence of the average saw-log and he can
no doubt enjoy anything. And now with this illumina-

tion of the subject you will better understand why I say
I was bored.

This is manuscript paper and I think it is perfectly
plain. Otherwise, several editors would by this time have
tomahawked me. Your paragraph relating to the tangle
of my letters was a remarkable case of supreme and un-
daunted assurance. I have been patiently and humbly
working at your pages, fitting them this way and that
way, trying them one way and then another, performing
puzzle solutions on them and exhausting half the devices
of the Chinese in efforts to form the proper sequence,
when, glory to you, along you come with an ingenuous
request to be more plain.

No, I know you are not cynical. But then you are very
tired. I am, too, very tired. So you think I am successful?
Well I don't know. Most people consider me successful.
At least, they seem to so think. But upon my soul I have
lost all appetite for victory, as victory is defined by the
mob. I will be glad if I can feel on my death-bed that
my life has been just and kind according to my ability
and that every particle of my little ridiculous stock of
eloquence and wisdom has been applied for the benefit
of my kind. From this moment to that deathbed may be
a short time or a long one but at any rate it means a life
of labor and sorrow. I do not confront it blithely. I confront it with desperate resolution. There is not even
much hope in my attitude. I do not even expect to do
good. But I expect to make a sincere, desperate, lonely
battle to remain true to my conception of my life and
the way it should be lived, and if this plan can accom-
plish anything, it shall be accomplished. It is not a fine
prospect. I only speak of it to people in whose opinions
I have faith. No woman has heard it until now.

When I speak of a battle I do not mean want, and
those similar spectres. I mean myself and the inherent

indolence and cowardice which is the lot of all men. I
mean, also, applause. Last summer I was getting very
ably laughed at for a certain book called The Black
Riders. When I was at my publishers yesterday I read
long extracts from English newspapers. I got an armful
of letters from people who declared that The Black
Riders was—etc, etc,—and then for the first time in my
life I began to be afraid, afraid that I would grow con-
tent with myself, afraid that willy-nilly I would be satis-
fied with the little, little things I have done. For the first
time I saw the majestic forces which are arrayed against
man's true success—not the world—the world is silly,
changeable, any of it's decisions can be reversed—but
man's own colossal impulses more strong than chains,
and I perceived that the fight was not going to be with
the world but with myself. I had fought the world and
had not bended nor moved an inch but this other battle—
it is to last on up through the years to my grave and only
on that day am I to know if the word Victory will look
well upon lips of mine.

It is a pretty solemn thing to talk thus and if you were
not you, I would re-write that paragraph and write it
much better but I know you will understand. To become
frank still further, it seems to me that I like you won-
derfully more, after confessing so unreservedly.

Dont trouble to locate Button. As I said, it was originally merely an expedient.

I am a very hurried writer but I hope my innumerable
editings will not make you impatient.

I don't like to appear common-place but I remember
that Button had your photograph and it seems to me that
one who pays you such such [sic] reserved and unre-
served, conditional and unconditional devotion as do I,
might be one of the chosen. If you refuse, I shall go and
slay Button for his impertinence.

I remain in the hope that you will do it. And remember that you are supposed to reply at once to this letter.

Yours sincerely

Stephen Crane

Sunday
Hartwood, N. Y.

FIVE

To Nellie Crouse, February 5, [1896]

The "about four new books coming out" must have been *A Souvenir and a Medley; George's Mother*, published in New York in June and later the same month in London; and the Appleton *Maggie* in June; *The Third Violet* may have been the fourth (cf. Crane to the Editor of *The Critic*, February 15, 1896, in Stallman, p. 647).

Hartwood, N. Y.

Dear Miss Crouse: Your photograph came today. Of course you know how very grateful I am to you. I had expected to hear from you on Monday but that day as well as Tuesday were times of disaster. At noon today, however the coming of the portrait relieved me. I am sure now, still more, that you are precisely the kind of young woman I have judged you. However, you have awed me. Yes, indeed, I am awed. There is something in your face which tells that there are many things which you perfectly understand which perhaps I don't under-

stand at all. This sounds very vague but it is nevertheless
very vague in my mind. I think it means that I am a savage. Of course I am admittedly a savage. I have been
known as docile from time to time but only under great
social pressure. I am by inclination a wild shaggy bar-
barian. I know that I am hopelessly befogging my meaning but then at best my meaning is a dim thing. I intend
to say at any rate that the light of social experience in
your eyes somewhat terrifies this poor outer pagan.

Well, it is better that I should gibber in the above
lines. Otherwise I would have bored you with long de-
scriptions of how charming I think the portrait.

I am engaged in rowing with people who wish me to
write more war-stories. Hang all war-stories. Nevertheless I submitted in one case and now I have a daily battle
with a tangle of facts and emotions. I am however doing
the thing in a way that is not without a mild satisfaction
for me.

I believe I told you in my last chronicle—my letters
arise almost to the dignity of chronicles; they are so long
—that I might go over to England on the 29th. Well, I've
almost given up the plan. The publishers and things in
London seem anxious for me to come, and people on this
side furnish me with unlimited introductions. So the
journey seems so easy and simple that I am quite out of
the humor of it. I dont think I shall go on until next
fall. Do you come east in the summer? I hope so. I never
work in the summer. It is one long lazy time to fool
away. Just now we in Hartwood are being drearily
snowed upon. Sometimes I am much agitated at the
thought that perhaps the little train won't be able to
struggle up the mountain and deliver my mail. As yet
however nothing has happened to it. Did not you once
ask me if Hartwood is out of the world? It is—very

much. New York is only 104 miles but it is a terrible 104 miles, and the mail service is wretched.

I have about four new books coming out. Sometimes I feel like sitting still and watching them appear. However, they are not good enough to delight me at all.

I wonder if you have a copy of *The Black Riders*. If you have not, let me know. I might as well let you know the worst of me at once. Although *Maggie* perhaps is the worst—or the most unconventional—of me.

I hope you will keep me no longer in anxiety by not writing. Of course I know that if you sent the picture you wouldn't write, and if you wrote, you wouldn't send the picture. So, possessing the picture I can forego the letter this week. Early next week, however, I shall not be so submissive. To add to the situation, no mail route, I imagine, can be so laboriously intricate as the way between Akron and Hartwood.

Yours sincerely

Stephen Crane

SIX

To Nellie Crouse, February 11, [1896]

The following story from the New York *Daily Tribune* for April 26, 1894, illumines Crane's reference to Sherry's:

THEY READ FROM UNPUBLISHED STORIES

The small ballroom at Sherry's was filled with a brilliant company on Saturday evening, who were guests of the Uncut Leaves Society at its last reading of the season. The guest of honor was Mrs. Frances Hodgson Burnett, who read in New York for the first time. Her selection was from an unfinished

novel. She was beautifully dressed in white silk, garnished with
mousseline-de-soie, and a corsage bunch of violets.

Miss Kate Jordan read an unpublished story entitled "Conrad Reuter of Second-ave," a story of the German quarter.
Gilbert Parker, of London, read one of his own stories, called
"The Great Slave Lake." John D. Barry read several unnamed
poems from the pen of Stephen Crane, who, according to Mr.
Barry, was too modest to read them himself; in fact, the poet
made the assertion that he "would rather die than do it."
L. J. B. Lincoln, the originator of the society, occupied the
chair.

Among the guests were Mrs. Edmund Clarence Stedman,
Arthur Stedman, Mrs. Richard Henry Stoddard, J. M. Stod-
dard, Mrs. Sargent, Judge and Mrs. Dillon, Mr. and Mrs.
George Haven Putnam, Mrs. Mary Mapes Dodge, Mr. and
Mrs. Nelson Wheatcroft, Count Von Rosen, Mrs. C. A. Dore-
mus, W. G. Maxwell, Mr. and Mrs. C. H. Young, Dr. and
Mrs. Frank Fuller, Mrs. Gustave Frohman and Mr. Hubert.

For some of the background to Crane's ideas of "the man of
fashion" and "the real aristocrat" see E. H. Cady, *The Gentleman in America*, Syracuse, 1949.

[No salutation]

Wherever that letter went is more than I can imagine.
It certainly never reached Hartwood. I am grieved at the
prospect of never seeing it but I console myself a little
with the remembrance that you wrote it. There is some
consolation in that, you know.

Your recent confession that in your heart you like the
man of fashion more than you do some other kinds of
men came nearer to my own view than perhaps you expected. I have indeed a considerable liking for the man of
fashion if he does it well. The trouble to my own mind
lies in the fact that the heavy social life demands one's
entire devotion. Time after time, I have seen the social

lion turn to a lamb and fail—fail at precisely the moment when men should not fail. The world sees this also and it has come to pass that the fashionable man is considerably jeered at. Men who are forever sitting with immovable legs on account of a tea-cup are popularly supposed to be worth little besides. This is true in the main but it is not without brave exceptions, thank heaven. For my part, I like the man who dresses correctly and does the right thing invariably but, oh, he must be more than that, a great deal more. But so seldom is he anymore than correctly-dressed and correctly-speeched, that when I see a man of that kind I usually put him down as a kind of an idiot. Still, as I have said, there are exceptions. There are men of very social habits who nevertheless know how to stand steady when they see cocked revolvers and death comes down and sits on the back of a chair and waits. There are men of very social habits who know good music from bad, good poetry from bad—(a few of 'em)—good drama from bad—(a very few of 'em)—good painting from bad. There are very many of them who know good claret and good poker-playing. There are a few who can treat a woman tenderly not only when they feel amiable but when she most needs tender-treatment. There many who can ride, swim, shoot and sail a boat, a great many. There are an infinitismal [sic] number who can keep from yapping in a personal way about women. There are a large number who refuse to haggle over a question of money. There are one or two who invariably mind their own business. There are some who know how to be frank without butchering the feelings of their friends. There is an enormous majority who, upon being insured of safety from detection—become at once the most unconventional of peoples.

In short they are precisely like the remainder of the race, only they devote their minds to riding smoothly.

A slight jolt gives them the impression that a mountain has fallen upon them.

I swear by the real aristocrat. The man whose fore-fathers were men of courage, sympathy and wisdom, is usually one who will stand the strain whatever it may be. He is like a thorough-bred horse. His nerves may be high and he will do a lot of jumping often but in the crises he settles down and becomes the most reliable and enduring of created things.

For the hordes who hang upon the out-skirts of good society and chant 143 masses per day to the social gods and think because they have money they are well-bred—for such people I have a scorn which is very deep and very intense. These people think that polite life is some-thing which is to be studied, a very peculiar science of which knowledge is only gained by long practice whereas what is called "form" is merely a collection of the most rational and just of laws which any properly-born person understands from his cradle. In Hartwood I have a great chance to study the new-rich. The Hartwood Club-house is only three miles away and there are some of the new rich in it. May the Lord deliver me from having social aspirations.

I can stand the society man, if he don't [sic] interfere with me; I always think the society girl charming but the type that I cant endure is the society matron. Of course there are many exceptions but some I have seen struck me afar off with the peculiar iron-like quality if their thick-headedness and the wild exuberance of their vanity.

On two or three occasions I had some things read at Sherry's and later by chance met people who had been there. I distinctly remember some compliments paid me very graciously and confidently by a woman. Nothing so completely and serenely stupid have I ever witnessed.

And the absolutely false tongue of her prattled away for ten minutes in more lies than are usually heard at one time. Of course it was nothing to me if she liked my stuff and it was nothing to her. She was merely being [sic] because she indifferently thought it to be correct at that moment, but how those old cats can stand up and lie until there is no breath left in them. Now, they think that is form, mind you, but, good heavens, it isnt. They think that a mere show of complacent idiocy is all that is necessary to a queen of society. Form really is truth, simplicity; when people surround it with falsity, interpret it as meaning: "lies," they become not society leaders but barbarians, savages, beating little silly tom-toms and flourishing little carved wooden goblins. They really defy every creed of this social god, the very diety [sic] which they worship.

I am rather apprehensive. I detest dogma and it strikes me that I have expressed too many opinions in this letter. When I express an opinion in writing I am in the habit of considering a long time and then formulating it with a great deal of care. This letter however has been so hasty that I have not always said precisely what I intended to say. But at any rate I hope it will be plain that I strongly admire the social God [sic] even if I do despise many of his worshippers.

As for the man with the high aims and things—which you say you like in your soul—but not in your heart—I dont know that he is to my mind any particular improvement on the society man. I shouldn't care to live in the same house with him if he was at all in the habit of talking about them. I get about two letters a day from people who have high literary aims and everywhere I go I seem to meet five or six. They strike me as about the worst and most penetrating kind of bore I know. Of course I, with my meagre successes, would feel like an

awful duffer if I was anything but very, very considerate
of them but it is getting to be a task. Of course that is
not the kind you meant. Still they are certainly people of
high aims and there is a ridiculous quality to me in all
high ambitions, of men who mean to try to make themselves great because they think it would [sic] so nice
to be great, to be admired, to be stared at by the mob.
"Well," you say, "I didnt mean that kind of high aim
either." Tolstoy's aim is, I suppose—I believe—to make
himself good. It is an incomparably quixotic task for any
man to undertake. He will not succeed; but he will even
succeed more than he can ever himself know, and so at
his nearest point to success he will be proportionally
blind. This is the pay of this kind of greatness.

This letter is certainly not a conscience-smiter but I
hope you will reply to it at the same length that you
claim for the lost letter.

I may go to Chicago in late February or early March
—over the Erie's lines. I wish you would tell me more
about your European trip. By the way, if you forbid me
going over on the same boat, it must be because you
think I am not clever.

Yours sincerely

Hartwood
Feb. 11th   Stephen Crane

SEVEN
To Nellie Crouse, March 1 and 18, [1896]

Crane got to Washington on a brief, abortive project of McClure's to have him do a book on "political society," apparently an ill-advised effort to convert Crane into a Lincoln Steffens. The shift in tone and the ultimate posture of permanent despair here are illuminated by three letters contemporaneous with this. On February 29 Crane wrote a confiding and philosophic letter to an old flame, Lily Brandon Munroe, about "the beautiful war" in which he had enlisted on the side of the Howellsian realists against the "romanticists" (cf. Melvin Schoberlin, ed., *The Sullivan County Sketches of Stephen Crane*, Syracuse, 1949, p. 19); the letter to Viola Allen on March 15, gaily recalling pre-school lights-o'-love is hardly a "flagons of despair" screed. And on the same day he wrote to Willis Hawkins, apologizing for some apparent personal slight with the typically masculine formula: "It was a woman! Don't you see? . . . I am sure, of course that you have been very much offended but it is a woman, I tell you, and I want you to forgive me." (Stallman, p. 649.)

33 East 22d, NYC
March 1st

[No salutation]

Do you know, I have succeeded in making a new kind of an idiot of myself. They had a winter party at Hartwood and after I had sat before twelve fire-places and drank 842 cups of tea, I said: "I shall escape." And so I

have come to New York. But New York is worse. I am
in despair. The storm-beaten little robin who has no
place to lay his head, does not feel so badly as do I. It
is not that people want to meet me. When that happens
I can endure it. But it is that mine own friends feel bit-
terly insulted if I do not see them twelve times a day—in
short they are all prepared to find me grown vain.

You know what I mean. That disgraceful Red Badge
is doing so very well that my importance has widened
and everybody sits down and calmly waits to see *me be
a chump*.

Dear me, how much am I getting to admire graveyards
—the calm unfretting unhopeing end of things—serene ab-
sence of passion—oblivious to sin—ignorant of the ac-
cursed golden hopes that flame at night and make a man
run his legs off and then in the daylight of experience
turn out to be ingenious traps for the imagination. If
there is a joy of living I cant find it. The future? The
future is blue with obligations—new trials—conflicts. It
was a rare old wine the gods brewed *for mortals*. Flagons
of despair—

———————

Washington, D. C.
March 18

Really, by this time I should have recovered enough to
be able to write you a sane letter but I cannot—my pen is
dead. I am simply a man struggling with a life that is no
more than a mouthful of dust to him.

                                        Yours sincerely

                                        Stephen Crane

The Cosmos Club
Washington

III APPENDICES

APPENDIX ONE

Stephen Crane at Syracuse University

I

Apparently in an effort to recapture as much of her husband's past as possible, Cora Crane wrote to Syracuse University soon after his death and received the following answer from Latin Professor Frank Smalley, one of the pillars of the faculty:

Syracuse, N. Y., Aug. 2, 1900

Dear Mrs. Crane:

Your letter making inquiries about Mr. Crane's connection with Syracuse University has just reached me. Our records show that he entered the University in 1890 as a member of the Class of '94. I do not think he remained the first year through although he may have done so, the records do not show that, nor do they show that he came to us from Lafayette College which I remember he did. He doubtless left Syracuse in the Spring of 1891. I knew him well. I have been a member of the Faculty here since 1874 and being a ΔY and the first graduate of that fraternity here the boys in the fraternity look upon me as a sort of father of the fraternity or chapter here. Mr. Crane was a ΔY and a brother brought him to my residence one evening soon after he entered and I conversed with him a long time. He was not inclined to be very studious and I find he has credit in only one subject and in that he has our highest mark, of course that study is English literature. He devoted himself to athletic sports with ardor, especially base-ball and was our finest player. His mother felt considerable anxiety about him and wrote me several letters. We looked upon him as an

57

exceedingly bright young man, of large capacity. He
would not be cramped by following a course of study he
did not care for. That is the secret of his few credits on
the books.

We are proud of his connection with this University.
I was not surprised to learn of his great work and that
he had won for himself imperishable fame, and I read his
writings with a feeling of almost paternal pride.

I suggest the following names of persons who remem-
ber him and doubtless can give you facts of interest:
Prof. C. J. Little, Evanston, Ill.—Prof. of history when
Mr. Crane was here. Prof. J. Scott Clark, Evanston, Ill.,
—Prof. of English here in '90. Principal W. H. Perry,
Lowville, N. Y., who first brought him to my residence.
George H. Bond, Syracuse, N. Y. who knows his athletic
record. These, perhaps, can suggest others.

We have given in our Alumni Record some space to
Mr. Crane.

Write me freely if I can be of further service to you.

Sincerely,

Frank Smalley

Latin

The tone of that letter is personally warm beyond the call of
duty or convention, especially as conventions were at the turn
of the century. None of the chilly rejection or uncomprehen-
sion which Crane has often been supposed to have received
from his colleges appears in it. And, indeed, very little of that
actually appears among the fairly extensive records of Crane's
brief semester at Syracuse which form a part of the University's Crane Collection. As a "special student," Crane had from
the start declared his unwillingness to stand for a degree and so

acquired privileges of course selection, even of non-attend-
ance, which fitted his cavalier notions of academic discipline.
So proceeding, he may well have irritated some professors and
shocked some classmates. But he was liked and admired by the
fraternity brothers who knew him well and by the boys on the
baseball club. And he was far from completely alienated from
the faculty.

On February 6, 1899, almost in the last year of his life, for
instance, he wrote from England to re-establish contact with
Dr. Charles J. Little, professor of history and logic who had
left Syracuse at the same time as Crane, to go to the Garrett
Biblical Institute, of which he finally became President (1895–
1910). The letter to Little (Stallman, pp. 685-687) is typical of
Crane. It expresses a candid if somewhat prickly gratitude to
Little for having once called him up, recognizing his unusual-
ness, to advise him kindly not to waste his life like a similar
young "John" whom Little had taught at Dickinson College.
The answer must have intrigued Crane: it is so much like Crane
himself and so little like the stereotype of a Victorian professor with which Crane's biographers have supposed he had to
do:

Evanston, Illinois
Feb. 23, 1899

Dear Mr. Crane:

"John" of whom you write was a clever lad, quite capable of writing "silly books"; if he had not hurried
quite so fast, in his eagerness "to tread the floors of hell."
As I remember "John" he was a young Apollo, lithe,
vigorous, handsome; if you reminded me of him, I must
have discerned in you potencies of various kinds and

feared that they might end in blight as "John" did. The
ruin of "John" that you recall to me is still a poignant
recollection; I should be glad to be quit of all responsibility for it. We teachers, I fear, handle life rather care-
lessly and "John's" blood has not yet ceased crying from
the ground. Well! I am glad you have kept to the high-
way. There are so many cross-cuts to hell, that I wonder
always when a full-blooded adventurous lad gets safely
established on the main road.

But you must be in error at one point. I surely did not
talk to you of "crime." For I know of no reason for my
doing so. Crime is rather an ugly word. Indeed my pen
balks at it now. And besides that, my impressions, I
fancy, came rather from what I saw than from what I
had heard. The resemblance to "John" quite probably
aroused forebodings and led to interpretations of expression and bearing that the future has not wholly discred-
ited. For I dealt rather with what might than with what
must be. And the "silly books" of which you speak so
disparingly [sic] and, yet with proper pride, have not
concealed the "might be" altogether. At least so it seems
to me who know them slightly. It amuses me, grey-
headed fellow that I am, to hear an artist talk of crime.
He, of all men, never knows it. He is taken up much with
its picturesque aspects. He knows how to use the criminal, actual or potential; but in order to use him, he de-
naturalizes, derealizes him. The words are vile enough;
but they alone will say just about what I mean. And this
he does in the *very instant of perception*. In his eagerness
to portray, he changes form and color, while he looks,
and never sees men and women as they are. It is, I fancy,
different with men whose knowledge of crime begins
with the sorrow that it causes. Mine began, in this wise,
very early. My earliest recollections are of crime and its
consequences. For me it has no picturesque aspects; al-

though it may, like a cancer, have picturesque associa-
tions. True, my knowledge of it is limited by the sources
from which I have drawn it—an unpleasantly large and
various assortment of family skeletons, and early and
dangerous acquaintance with the slums of Bedford St.
and St. Mary St. in Philada., the revelation of the criminal court, the Reformatory and the Insane Asylum; but
above all from the perpetual study of the criminal that
escapes the jail and seems to escape, in this world, the
judgement of God. Add to this a fairly large acquaintance
with the memoirs of men and women who have sinned
in many languages and through many centuries. Of
course, this kind of knowledge is a form of ignorance.
To know poison, one must have it in one's blood. And
even then, the experimenter encounters a peculiar difficulty; the poison destroys his power to perceive its effects. And I am glad to learn that your knowledge of
crime is not of this sort. You see, too, that I would not
over-value it, if it were; I should still insist upon "cor-
recting the compass" before trusting wholly to its indica-
tions. It pleases me to sit at your fireside, invisibly, and
to be talked about, as I appear to your kindly imagination. I have no share in anything that you have done or
won. Many, indeed, are the influences that make and
save a soul. It is barely possible that the moan of my
early experiences and later sorrows vibrated through
my clumsy speech and awkward thinkings and gave
them a touch of enduring pathos. This, I fancy, rather
than any words of mine has survived in your memory,
and it pleases me to have it so. The best of our books are
"silly" and our knowledge vanishes away. But love never
faileth. And, therefore, if a face should haunt me tomorrow as yours did aforetime, I shall speak as I did then,
wisely or foolishly, as the thoughts may bubble up within
my brain. You younger men are what you will be,—

sometimes, at least; we older men, alas, must be, what we are. We have exhausted our chances; and there are no more tickets for the transformation baths on sale.

Yours very truly,

Charles J. Little

II

The connection of preacher's son Stephen Crane with Syracuse University was not accidental. His first few days in town he spent with his mother's aunt-by-marriage, the widow of Bishop Jesse T. Peck, one of the founders of the University. Then he moved with joy into the fraternity house (the only one then on campus) of Delta Upsilon, into which he had been initiated at Lafayette the preceding Fall. He was a faithful member, missing only four chapter meetings out of twenty-four between January and June, and those just prior to base-ball games. He was writing correspondence for the New York *Tribune* and, tradition says, for the Detroit *Free Press*. Therefore some of his days were spent in police court or the railroad station, watching the stream of humanity flow past, rather than up on The Hill with textbooks. He made the most of his status as "special student."

The liveliest glimpses of Crane at Syracuse, together with a dramatic picturization of the Philistine Dinner and Willis Hawkins, have come from the pen of his classmate Frank W. Noxon, himself an effective journalist.

706 Otis Bldg.,
Washington, D. C.
Dec. 7, 1926

Mr. Max J. Herzberg, Pres.,
The Stephen Crane Assn.,
Newark Evening News,
Newark, New Jersey

My dear Mr. Herzberg:—

One of Stephen Crane's characteristics was a haunting solicitude for the comfort and welfare of other people, especially those of narrow opportunity. He thought about it as one thinks about an art or craft, developing a style and inventing original methods.

My acquaintance with him began at Syracuse University, where we were in the Class of '94 and in the Delta Upsilon Fraternity, which Crane had joined at La Fayette earlier in the year. The earliest thing I remember concerning him was an essay which he read one night in chapter meeting on some serious political subject related to Russia. I saw the manuscript and in conversation later exclaimed at its exquisite legibility. This astonished me in a daily newspaper reporter such as Crane had already been. He replied that from the outset of his writing he had kept in mind the compositor, whose earnings depended upon the amount he could set, and this in turn upon the time it took to read the copy.

Among his favorite objects of solicitude were dogs. He loved them and was beloved by them. He embraced without question the well-known theory, which I had then never heard before, that the instinctive attitude of a dog toward a new human acquaintance was an infallible test of character, and that no man who felt repugnance or

even indifference toward canines, familiar or casual, could
be wholly trusted for a kind heart toward those of his
own species. Crane wrote of a dog named Jack; and I distinctly recall the fondness he showed for a story about
this Jack, which he let me read. The St. Nicholas magazine returned it, explaining that too many good dog stories were already in hand, but speaking in complimentary
terms. I got the impression that Stephen regarded this as
friendly not only to him but to the dog; and his gratitude
in literary defeat had a note of affectionate pride.

No doubt some of our acquaintances in those days as
well as critics and readers since had ascribed Crane's interest in unfortunate women to another instinct than sympathy and compassion. Nobody can be sure. But knowing him pretty well and seeing him a good deal in the
company of girls, toward whom he showed respect and
deference, I have no difficulty in believing that when he
wrote about scarlet sisters or vehemently defended one as
later he did in a New York police court, the dominant
impulse was a desire to serve the helpless. "Maggie, a Girl
of the Streets," at least in its early form, was wholly or
in part written at Syracuse. With typical carelessness the
author left the sheets lying about in the front corner room
which he shared with Clarence Norton Goodwin. Some
of these pages were picked up and read by droppers-in.
The other day a '93 man whom I had not seen for many
years asked me what I thought of Crane as a man at the
time, knowing that he was writing that sort of thing. Had
it been my observation, as it had been his, that Crane's
own conduct seemed to contrast with his choice of literary themes? In 1926 this sounds primitive. It was 1890,
and it was a Syracuse much more Methodist and very
much more "divinity" than now. By the way, in after
years Crane told me about the publication of "Maggie."
He had vainly peddled it among the publishers, though

to his delight the gentle realist, Howells, reading it for somebody [Harpers?] had written an enthusiastic memorandum. Finally he paid for bringing it out himself, using the pseudonym "Johnston Smith." The cover was yellow paper with the title in large black letters. Four men were hired to sit all day one in front of another in New York elevated trains, reading intently and holding up the volume so that passengers would think the metropolis was "Maggie"-mad.

With his Catholic taste in people Crane in our day combined considerable sense of social form. At the fraternity house one function was an annual party to which every co-ed on the hill was invited, the requisite number of partners being recruited from our chapters at other Central New York colleges. For the party in Crane's one winter with us, after getting into his own evening dress he went about the house with a box of shirt studs and a punch, detecting local brethren whose well starched bosoms were innocent both of studs and of holes and rectifying the deficiency.

Crane was brave, physically, morally and socially. Nothing would do, therefore, but he must pity the coward and try to understand him. So we got "The Red Badge of Courage." Incidentally, the use of the word "Red" in this title was part of a program. After the book appeared he and I had somewhere a talk about color in literature. He told me that a passage in Goethe analyzed the effect which the several colors have upon the human mind. Upon Crane this had made a profound impression and he had utilized the idea to produce his effects. Do you remember the colors of the burning chemicals in "The Monster"? There you had them all at once.

Most of us were surprised, though we needn't have been, when this lover of his kind got into a war. It is well remembered how the description of Chancellorsville in

"The Red Badge," written by a youth not born until
1871, stirred the Civil War veterans and singled out the
author as the one sure-fire war correspondent should war
come. War came—with Spain; and Mr. Hearst's people
annexed Crane for Cuba. The next fall, driving in a "hack"
from Boston to Cambridge, where he was reporting a foot-
ball game, Crane in the intervals between those harrowing
coughs which got him in the end told me about Santi-
ago. He said he was of no use whatever. The moment the
fighting began Crane started carrying buckets of water
to the wounded and paid no attention whatever to the
observation necessary for writing newspaper despatches.

Not even Crane, love him as most men did, was always
able to command from others that tolerance which he dif-
fused so infinitely. At our era, security against nicotine
was still a hope to which a he-man might aspire. The heat-
ing system in the chapter house carried smoke from one
room to another. Whether the brethren (assaying then
pretty high in divinity students) were more annoyed and
alarmed at having to inhale attenuated whiffs so penetrating to their castles, or concerned for the salvation of the
smokers, the iron heel descended, and an unregenerate
group captained by the grinning Crane and consisting of
Goodwin, Congdon, and perhaps others (I never smoked
until I was 50 but often went along) were translated to the
cupola, where on freezing days in ulsters, ear-laps, mit-
tens and arctics they exhaled the fumes unsmelt to heaven.
Some years ago in Northampton, Mass., I visited F. K.
Congdon, who was, and I suppose is, superintendent of
schools there. Congdon with a Sherlock Holmes air
wanted to know whether in 1907 I was an editorial writer
on the Boston Herald. I was, and his clue had been an
article on Crane mentioning the cupola smoker, which
Congdon said no other newspaper man could have known
about.

If you go to East Aurora you will see on exhibition handwriting and other souvenirs of Crane, but Crane was one of the series who were driven from Elbert Hubbard by what they believed was Hubbard's abuse of them. In 1893 or thereabouts, soon after I went to Boston, Hubbard ended by his and the Dean's mutual consent his short sojourn at Harvard, leaving behind him among other things an unexpired rental on a Cambridge post-office box, to which subscriptions and contributions might be sent for a new magazine called The Philistine. It seems that one Bickford and one Taber (with the latter of whom I became intimate and enjoy to this day quinquennial reunions) for a brief while in Denver, where they worked on the Times, published a Philistine. When Hubbard quit the soap business for literature he did not instantly acquire either that classic appearance or that confidence in his pen which subsequently amazed all the continents, so he took on a series of editors, of whom Taber was first. Taber proposed the revival of the Philistine. Not knowing these worthies, but dwelling in Boston and noting the Cambridge address, which made them seem near, although already they were in fact far away in East Aurora, I sent them some piece of nonsense about a character named Clangingharp, which was published, and an acquaintance begun by mail with both Taber and Hubbard. Presently Crane appeared likewise among the contributors. A by-law of the Society of the Philistines published on the magazine cover prescribed a duty of members to attend the annual dinner. Some years went by without the first annual dinner, but about 1895 it was announced that the annual dinner was coming off with Crane as guest of honor. Borrowing money and probably clothes, I made the journey to Buffalo, where the feed was held at the Genesee House. There must have been 15 or 20 there, most of us freaks or near-freaks, and on the menu were scriptures by others who couldn't come but admired the guest. Hubbard, still timid, sat at the foot of the table and Taber at the head; Crane on Taber's right; Claude Fayette Bragdon (who these days without the Fayette designs scenic and costume investiture for theatrical productions) on his left, with me next; and on Crane's right, Willis W. Hawkins, Editor then of Brains. Hawkins borrowed cuff links of me which I never got back.

After dinner Taber rose and began his speech. "Probably," he said, "the most unique—" That was as far as he got. A voice somewhere down toward Hubbard called out "Can 'unique' be compared?" This was the signal. It determined the tone of the festivities. In the best Clover and Gridiron manner Taber and all the other speakers were guyed and ragged from start to finish. Crane, having the time of his life, was called up, and they had as much fun with him as with the others.

When Crane sat down up rose Claude Bragdon. After 31 years I can still hear the sound of his voice and see the look on his face. "I came here," he said, "to do honor to Stephen Crane, not to ridicule him. I regret to take this step, but I cannot longer remain in the room." The door was on the far side of the table. To get out, Bragdon had to walk around behind Taber and Crane. Hawkins stood and blocked him. "One moment," he said. "I am the oldest man in this room. I know Stephen Crane better than anyone else here. I have slept with him, eaten with him, starved with him, ridden with him, swum with him. I know him through and through, every mood. I have come here, like our friend, to do honor to Stephen Crane. I have taken part in all that has occurred, and he knows I love him and admire him. He knows that you all do. I assure you he feels more complimented by the spirit of this meeting than he would have been by all the solemn eulogies that could be pronounced." Crane was nodding his head off. Everybody applauded.

"I am sorry," said Bragdon, "if I have made a mistake. I ask your pardon."

"Pardon is granted you," Hawkins answered, "on one condition."

Bragdon looked up inquiringly.

"That condition," said Hawkins, "is that you turn around and take your seat."

And Bragdon did it.

I never knew the particular circumstances under which in Crane's case the author, like so many others, fell out with Hubbard, but have always assumed that it was the Fra's democratic prejudice against royalties. Whatever the reason, the inevitable assault appeared in the Philistine, and in Crane's case it was no less than a serious and circumstantial narrative of his having been "drowned in the Irish Sea," though Crane considerably survived this obituary.

Yours truly,

Frank W. Noxon

III

Normally enough, Crane published a rudimentary tale, "The King's Favor," in *The University Herald*, a student publication, on May 11, 1891 and followed it up the next year, despite his departure from campus, with "The Cry of the Huckleberry Pudding" for the December 23, 1892, issue. The editors then also took space to notice with pride that his placing of "A Tent in Agony" in the December *Cosmopolitan* made "Mr. Crane . . . the youngest writer whose productions have ever appeared in that magazine." Mr. Noxon's letter records the persistent but unverifiable legend that he had begun *Maggie* in his room in the Delta Upsilon house.

But baseball was his true love at Syracuse. At Claverack and Lafayette he had been a catcher, disdaining the heavy mitt just then coming into use and handling fast pitching with nothing but a piece of pig-skin across his battered left hand. His slender 120 pounds were often bounced backward when the pitcher burned one in. Grit and a fierce competitive spirit made him the inevitable leader of the Syracuse team, but he and they had all to face up to his one serious handicap as a catcher. Neither strong nor heavy enough to whip the ball on a line down to

Crane and the Syracuse Baseball team of 1891

second base on an attempted steal by the runner from first, he had to dash forward and wind up before he could make the throw. He developed ingenious variations on the "pick-off play" to counter his weakness, but too many bases were stolen against him. In mid-season he moved to shortstop, where his speed and competitiveness made him a complete success. He was an effective batsman, though never, of course, a "long-ball hitter," and a fast, dangerous base-runner. His college team won fifteen of its twenty-four games and placed third in the Intercollegiate Baseball Association made up of teams from Colgate, Hamilton, Hobart, Rochester, Syracuse, and Union.

The college annual for 1892, *The Onondagan*, listed in traditional style Crane's other interests and activities in the college:

> Member of the class of 1894, Syracuse chapter of
>   Delta Upsilon
> Member and secretary-treasurer of the Claverack
>   College and Hudson River Institute Alumni Asso-
>   ciation at Syracuse
>
> Member of the Tooth-Pick Club, Delta Upsilon House
>   [the fraternity boarding club]
> Member of the Delta Upsilon Coasting Club
> Captain of the Delta Upsilon Cricket Club.

The equally traditional humor of the annual put Crane's name in a column headed "Grinds" and faced it with a quotation presumably bent on student irony:

> Sweet drop of pure and pearly light,
> In thee the rays of virtue shine,
> More calmly clear, more mildly bright
> Than any gem that gilds the mine.

Nevertheless, the baseball season done, he left the campus for good in the early summer of 1891.

It would be as rash to say precisely what Stephen Crane got from his semester at Syracuse as it would be to say that he got nothing. He retained a certain interest and affection for the place and some of the people he had known there. And certainly he became a legend on the campus almost immediately. Student publications reprinted as their own "The Cry of the Huckleberry Pudding" in 1897, 1909, and 1930; "The King's Favor" reappeared in 1901, 1921, and 1935. *The University Herald* followed him up in 1895 and 1896 as well as 1892, reviewing *The Red Badge* and *The Black Riders* and crowing over his success. Altogether at least twelve articles on him appeared in student publications between 1892 and 1900, the year of his death. Alumni of the college and of his fraternity have continued the interest from college generation to generation, eventually creating the University Library's Stephen Crane Collection as a tangible memorial of Stephen Crane at Syracuse.

Edith Carpenter Lundgren to Lester G. Wells, February, 1953

For its specific and very special information about Nellie Crouse and her relations with Crane, the following letter from Nellie Crouse's daughter is published.

> Mrs. Sven R. Lundgren
> Washington 7, D. C.

> Monday [February 1953]

Dear Mr. Wells:

Thank you so much for yours of the 10th. I enclose my mother's charming picture of herself taken the year before she married my father and I would appreciate it if you will return it at your leisure after you have had it photostated.

In answer to your questions.

1. Her full name was Nellie Janes Crouse.
2. Her home was in Akron, Ohio, where she was born.
3. She attended school at Mt. Vernon, Wash., D.C.
4. She married my father, Samuel Emlen Carpenter, June 16, 1897.
5. Mother had six children including myself
    My brother Samuel E. Carpenter 2nd.
    My twin sister Eleanor Longstreth Carpenter, married Jacques Dunant of Geneva, Switzerland (deceased).
    Another sister Mildred Douglas Carpenter married William Handy Ellicott of Baltimore, Md.

Another brother, Emlen Newbold Carpenter
died in infancy (1 year old).
Another brother died at birth, no name.

It is difficult to say if Mother was actually considering
marrying Crane or not. She was so beautiful and viva-
cious and had so many admirers that possibly it would be
safe to say she was considering marrying him, until my
father came along and was more successful in sweeping
her off her feet than Crane was. I do know I was brought
up on Crane's love for her and we as children were always fascinated by the romance. Yes! Crane did visit her
in Akron just before she married my father. She met my
father at a college prom at Harvard where he went to
college. They married in Akron, Ohio, and moved to
Ridgefield, Conn. where we were all born and lived until
1914 when their marriage broke up and mother returned
us all to Philadelphia, Pa. where the Carpenter family all
originally came from and she died there March 20, 1943.

If there are any further details you would like that I
have failed to mention do not hesitate to ask for them. . . .

Very sincerely

Edith Carpenter Lundgren

APPENDIX THREE

The George Arents Stephen Crane Collection at Syracuse
University

When Wharton Miller became director of the Syracuse University Library in 1927 he believed that for two reasons the library should have an extended and comprehensive Stephen Crane collection: first, because of Crane's importance as an American writer; second, because of Crane's presence at Syracuse as a student in the early months of 1891. By purchase and gifts the present collection at Syracuse has become one of the outstanding Crane collections in public ownership, supplementing notable collections at Columbia, Dartmouth and Yale. The collecting policy extends over three broadly-interpreted fields:

1. All writings of Crane in whatever form they have appeared and in whatever edition they have been published.
2. All critical and biographical materials about him by any author and in whatever form published, book or serial.
3. Manuscripts, letters, memorabilia, and ephemera.

The rarest items of the collection have been presented by Mr. George Arents of New York, bibliophile, donor of the Arents Tobacco Collection to the New York Public Library, and a member of the board of trustees of Syracuse University.

A few selected, choice items of the collection are listed below:

MANUSCRIPTS

" 'Ol' Bennet' & the Indians. A Tale of Wyoming Valley."
4 pages. Ink.

"A Desertion."

   2 pages. Pencil.

Fragment of the opening portion of a short story beginning
—"The door clanged behind him . . ."

"Fast rode the knight . . ." (Poem)

   1 page. Ink.

"What? You define me God with these trinkets? . . ." (Poem)

   1 page. Ink.

In Crane's holograph at bottom of page: "Oh, [Elbert] Hubbard, mark this well. Mark it well! If it is over-balancing
your discretion, inform me. S.C."

ORIGINAL LETTERS

1890. Between September 12 and November 27.

   S.C., #170 East Hall, Lafayette College (Easton, Pennsylvania)

     4 pages. Ink.

1891. January 9.

   S.C., Delta Upsilon Chapter House, Syracuse, N. Y., to
Odell S. Hathaway.

     1 page. Ink. Small portion missing.

1892. December 15.

   S.C., Lake View, New Jersey, to Lucius Lucine Button, 1064
Eastern Boulevard, New York City.

     3 pages. Ink.

Written on stationery of "Pendennis Club, 1064 Eastern Boulevard."

1894. December.
S.C., 33 East 22nd Street, [New York City], to Copeland and Day, Boston, Massachusetts.
  1 page. Ink.

Dear sirs:—It may be that I will be unable to reach Boston before I start for the west and if it so happens,—I should like to hear how the poems are coming on, anyway, and wether [sic] there is anything you would care to have my opinion about.

Sincerely yours
Stephen Crane

New York
Sturday [sic]

This letter concerns Crane's second published book—"The Black Riders and Other Lines" which Copeland and Day published in 1895. Although the letter bears no date, it is conjectured that it was written late in 1894 just before he left for the Southwest and Mexico in January of the following year. At approximately the conjectured date of this letter his *Red Badge* was being published serially in the Philadelphia *Press.*

1895. January 2.
S.C., 143 East 23rd Street, New York City, to Copeland and Day, Boston, Massachusetts.
  1 page. Ink.

Dear sirs: I return proof sheet instantly. I do not care for
a corrected proof. I go west so soon now that the proofs
will have to be hurried along or I can get to see but few
of them. I wish to know if some manner of announcement
card can be printed which I can send to my friends. I
think it would benefit matters greatly.

Yours sincerely
Stephen Crane

Copeland and Day

This concerns "The Black Riders" as does the letter preceding. Copyright was applied for January 14 and publication
was announced on May 11.

1895. February 19.
S.C., New Orleans, Louisiana, to Corwin Knapp Linson.
1 page. Ink.

1895. August 3.
S.C., Parker's Glen, Pike Co., Pennsylvania, to Karl Knortz,
Evansville, Indiana.
1 page. Ink.

Dear sir: I have requested the publishers to forward you
at once a copy of The Black Riders and I remain anxious
to see your frank opinion of it as expressed in the Leipsic
publication.

Sincerely yours
Stephen Crane

Karl Knortz (1841–1918) came from Germany to America in 1863. He had received the doctorate from Heidelberg the same year. He had translated Longfellow and Whittier into German and was a contributor to German literary periodicals. At the date of this letter he was head of the German department, public schools, in Evansville. It has been impossible to discover any German review of "The Black Riders."

1895. October.
S.C., Hartwood, Sullivan County, New York, to Willis Brooks Hawkins, New York.
3 pages. Ink.

1895. December 31.
S.C., Hartwood, New York, to Nellie Crouse, Akron, Ohio.
8 pages. Ink.
Clippings incorporated in letter: Printed invitation to Philistines dinner, dated November 10, 1895; p. 2. Printed copy of Crane's acceptance, dated November 15, suggesting December 19 as date of dinner; Undated newspaper account of the dinner from a Buffalo paper.

1896. January 6.
S.C., Hartwood, New York, to Nellie Crouse, Akron, Ohio.
9 pages. Ink.

1896. January 12.
S.C., Hartwood, New York, to Nellie Crouse, Akron, Ohio.
12 pages. Ink.

Clipping pasted to page 4 concerning *The Red Badge;* from an English newspaper.

1896. January (late).
S.C., Hartwood, New York, to Nellie Crouse, Akron, Ohio.
9 pages. Ink.

1896. February 5.
S.C., Hartwood, New York, to Nellie Crouse, Akron, Ohio.
6 pages. Ink.

1896. February 11.
S.C., Hartwood, New York, to Nellie Crouse, Akron, Ohio.
12 pages. Ink.

1896. March 1 and March 18.
S.C., 33 East 22nd Street, New York City, and Cosmos Club, Washington, D.C., to Nellie Crouse, Akron, Ohio.
4 pages. Ink.
The portion written from Washington is dated March 18.

1899. Autumn.
S.C., Brede Place, Brede, Sussex, England to James Pinker, London.
1 page. Ink.

Dear Pinker: I enclose Chapters XXIV and XXV (4000 wds) of the Romance for typing and also the remainder of the "A Swede's Campaign in Germany" article.

I understand you did not manage the cheque for £30. I sent my wife off to Paris with the money that my brother had sent to buy some clothes for my niece in Paris and my wife *must* get a draft on Monday. Cannot you send her by cable a draft for £20 on the Parisian correspondents of your bankers in London, and also send £10 to her a/c at Brown Shipley & Co? The poor things may be left high and dry in Paris.

My wife's address is "Hotel St. Petersbourg, Paris". I enclose a wire which I hope—I beg you to be able to send early Monday A.M.

The Romance will run very little beyond the 80000 words. Chap XXVI may reach you Tuesday.

Yours etc.

S. Crane

James Pinker was Crane's English literary agent and friend. This letter concerns two works which were published after Crane's death (June 5, 1900). The romance, *The O'Ruddy* was first published in New York late in 1903. The manuscript was completed by Robert Barr. A few days before the Cranes left England for the Continent in May, 1900, Cora Crane wrote Pinker that her husband would like to have Robert Barr complete the manuscript and she added—"perhaps Mr. Kipling may edit . . . You should get a big serial price . . ."

"A Swede's Campaign . . ." was an account of the battles of Leipzig and Lutzen and was included in "Great Battles of the World," first published in Philadelphia late in 1901.

Crane's niece, Helen, the daughter of his brother, William, was attending school in Switzerland.

(1900).   August 28. (no place)
Cora Crane to unidentified publisher.
   1 page. Ink.

Dear Sir:
   I am sending my friend Mrs. Bootherton(?) with the ms. "finished" of three stories of my late Husband's, Stephen Crane.
   I am begging that you will do the best that you can with them and that you will advance me £5—on them. I have just had a terrible run with the woman who keeps this place and must leave today. I am short just £3.10 in paying her. These things and kinds of people are new to me and I am unfit to go out or I would come personally to see you.

Faithfully yours
CORA CRANE

Although the letter bears no year, it is conjectured that it was written in 1900. Crane died in June of this year. The story " 'Ol' Bennet' and the Indians" was published in *Cassell's Magazine* in December 1900. Cora returned to Jacksonville, Florida in 1901, according to James Branch Cabell.

A SELECTION FROM THE PUBLISHED WRITINGS

Note. Williams-Starrett *Bibliography* * numbers have been included below. Of the seventy numbered items appearing in this bibliography, the Collection has sixty-four.

. . . . . .

Active Service . . . New York, 1899. WS 21; London, 1899. WS 22

A Battle in Greece. Mt. Vernon, N.Y., 1936. WS 40

Best Things from American Literature. New York, 1899. WS 24 (Includes *A Detail* and *A Tale of Mere Chance.*)

The Black Riders . . . Boston, 1895. WS 2, WS 2a, WS 2b; Boston, 1896. WS 2c; London, 1896. WS 11

The Blood of the Martyr. Mt. Vernon, N.Y., 1940. WS 41

Bowery Tales . . . London, 1900. WS 25

Collected Poems . . . New York, 1930. WS 39

Cry of the Huckleberry Pudding. In *University Herald.* Syracuse, N.Y., December 23, 1892; *University Herald.* Syracuse, N.Y., October, 1897; *Syracusan.* Syracuse, N.Y., January, 1909; *Chap Book.* Syracuse, N.Y., May, 1930.

Et Cetera: a Collector's Scrap Book. Chicago, 1924. WS 37 (Includes *At the Pit Door* and *The Great Boer Trek.*)

George's Mother. New York, 1896. WS 6; London, 1896. WS 32

Great Battles of the World. Philadelphia, 1901. WS 30; London, 1901. WS 32

Killing His Bear. (". . . printed for the friends of Lee and Gabriel Engel . . . 1949".)

---

* Williams, Ames W. and Starrett, Vincent. *Stephen Crane: a Bibliography.* Glendale, California, 1948. 161 pp.

The King's Favor. In *University Herald.* Syracuse, N.Y., May
11, 1891; *University Herald.* Syracuse, N.Y., April 11, 1901;
Phoenix (Literary Quarterly) Syracuse, N.Y., December,
1921; *Argot* (Literary Quarterly) Syracuse, N.Y., March,
1935.

The Lanthorn Book . . . New York, 1898. WS 19 (Includes
Wise Men, signed by Crane.)

Last Words. London, 1902. WS 33 and 33c

Legends. Ysleta, Texas, 1942. WS 46

Lines. Printed for the friends of Melvin H. Schoberlin. Balti-
more, 1947. WS 49

The Little Regiment . . . New York, 1896. WS 10 and 10a. (The
copy of 10a is inscribed in Crane's holograph—"To my
friend J. G. Widrig, USS Scorpion, from Stephen Crane.
Havana. Nov. 24, 1898".)

The Little Regiment . . . London, 1897. WS 12

A Lost Poem. 1932. Printed "for the friends of Harvey Taylor."
WS 45

Maggie: A Girl of the Streets. A Story of New York by Johnston Smith. New York, 1893. WS 1. Inscribed on front cover
—"To my friend Charles J. Pike. Stephen Crane. May 10th,
1896." Laid in is a holograph statement signed "Charles J.
Pike, Clinton, Connecticut, April 1, 1930" in which Mr. Pike
says that this was Crane's "own copy"; that Crane gave it to
him when they were living in Pike's studio "on the third
floor front of the old building . . . on the corner of 33rd
St. and 6th Ave."

Maggie . . . New York, 1896. WS 8, WS 8a; London, 1896.
WS 9

Men, Women, and Boats. New York, 1921. WS 36

The Monster . . . New York, 1899. WS 36; London, 1901. WS 31

The Open Boat . . . New York, 1898. WS 15; London, 1898. WS 16

The O'Ruddy . . . New York, 1903. WS 34; London, 1904. WS 35

Pictures of War. London, 1898. WS 17

Pike County Puzzle. Camp Interlaken, Penna., August 28, 1894. WS 43

The Public Papers of a Bibliomaniac . . . by Charles Honce, Mt. Vernon, N.Y., 1942. WS 42. (Includes Crane's newspaper account of the parade of the Junior Order of United American Mechanics, Asbury Park, N.J., 1892.)

The Red Badge of Courage . . . New York, 1895. WS 3; London, 1896. WS 4 and 4a

La Conquête du Courage. Paris, France, n.d. (before 1929); Paris, France, 1939. WS 117 (The collection contains 26 editions and variants of *The Red Badge* . . .)

A Souvenir and a Medley. East Aurora, N.Y., 1896. WS 5

Spanish-American War Songs . . . Detroit, Michigan, 1898. WS 18 (Contains the first printing of "The Blue Battalions" in book form.)

Sullivan County Sketches. Edited by Melvin Schoberlin. Syracuse University Press, 1949.

The Third Violet. New York, 1897. WS 13; London, 1897. WS 14 and 14a

Whilomville Stories. New York, 1900. WS 26a; London, 1900. WS 27

The Work of Stephen Crane. Edited by Wilson Follett. New York, 1925–1927. 12 vol. WS 38

Wounds in the Rain . . . New York, 1900. WS 28; London, 1900. WS 29

ITEMS RELATING TO STEPHEN CRANE AT SYRACUSE UNIVERSITY

Baseball used by him, Spring of 1891.

Group photograph of the Syracuse University baseball team, Spring of 1891, including him.

Photograph of inscription carved by him on wall of cupola of the Delta Upsilon fraternity house—"Sunset. 1891. Steph Crane".

Recollections (letters and manuscripts) of his classmates at Syracuse including M. J. French, Clarence Goodwin, Frederic M. Lawrence, Frank Noxon, Clarence L. Peaslee, *et al.*

Attendance records of Delta Upsilon, Spring of 1891, indicating a regular pattern of attendance by him at the weekly chapter meetings, except at those immediately prior to important baseball games in which he played. (NOTE: Property of the Syracuse Chapter of Delta Upsilon and deposited with the collection.)

Syracuse University student year book—*ONONDAGAN 1891* —with Crane mentioned.

Syracuse University student periodical articles concerning his life and works.

MISCELLANEA AND CURIOSA

Original Photographs

Four formal portraits taken by his friend, Corwin Knapp Linson.
Crane and L. L. Button on roof, New York, 1893, taken by
  C. K. L.
C. K. L. and Crane on roof, New York, 1893.
C. K. L. and Crane at coal mines, Scranton, Penna., 1893.
Three portraits of Cora Crane, one signed "Imogene Carter".
His residence at Brede Place and Oxted, England.
His birthplace, Newark, New Jersey.

.   .   .   .   .

Publishers' posters announcing C's literary productions.
Original etching by Constance Naar—portrait of Crane.
Program of the Philistines dinner in honor of Crane, East
  Aurora, New York, December 19, 1895.
Bronislau Kaper's original musical score for the MGM produc-
  tion of "The Red Badge ..." presented by Metro-Goldwyn-
  Mayer Pictures.
A Song Cycle from Stephen Crane's Black Riders by William
  Schuyler. St. Louis, 1900. WS 47
The Blade of Grass: for Voice and Piano by William Roy, New
  York, 1948.
Places among the Stars. Song ... by Roland Farley, New York,
  1933. WS 48

Syracuse University considers Stephen Crane an alumnus although his membership in the student body was of short duration. A special collection in the Syracuse University Library contains many items connected with Crane while a student at the University as well as during later years.

Edwin H. Cady is professor of English at Syracuse University. He is the author of *The Gentleman in America, Whittier on Writers and Writing*, and *Literature of the Early Republic*. Lester G. Wells is Curator of Special Collections, Syracuse University Library.

The book was designed by Gordon Paxson, formerly a member of the faculty of the School of Art, Syracuse University, now a free-lance designer and consultant.

Typesetting and binding is by The American Book–Stratford Press, New York City. Presswork is by The Salina Press, Syracuse, New York. The type face used is Janson linotype.